"DEATH TO THE WORLD" AND APOCALYPTIC THEOLOGICAL AESTHETICS

T&T Clark Explorations at the Crossroads of Theology and Aesthetics

Series editors
Anthony Godzieba
Jennifer Newsome Martin
Judith Gruber

Volume II

"DEATH TO THE WORLD" AND APOCALYPTIC THEOLOGICAL AESTHETICS

Robert Cady Saler

LONDON • NEW YORK • OXFORD • NEW DELHI • SYDNEY

T&T CLARK

Bloomsbury Publishing Plc, 50 Bedford Square, London, WC1B 3DP, UK
Bloomsbury Publishing Inc, 1359 Broadway, New York, NY 10018, USA
Bloomsbury Publishing Ireland, 29 Earlsfort Terrace, Dublin 2, D02 AY28, Ireland

BLOOMSBURY, T&T CLARK and the T&T Clark logo are
trademarks of Bloomsbury Publishing Plc

First published in Great Britain 2024
Paperback edition published 2026

Copyright © Robert Cady Saler, 2024

Robert Cady Saler has asserted his right under the Copyright,
Designs and Patents Act, 1988, to be identified as Author of this work.

For legal purposes the Acknowledgments on pp. xi–xii constitute an
extension of this copyright page.

Cover design: Ben Anslow
Cover image: Vintage engraving of the Gallery at Convent of St Catherine,
Sinai, 19th century (Contributor: duncan1890 / iStock)

All rights reserved. No part of this publication may be: i) reproduced or transmitted in
any form, electronic or mechanical, including photocopying, recording or by means of
any information storage or retrieval system without prior permission in writing from the
publishers; or ii) used or reproduced in any way for the training, development or operation
of artificial intelligence (AI) technologies, including generative AI technologies. The rights
holders expressly reserve this publication from the text and data mining exception as
per Article 4(3) of the Digital Single Market Directive (EU) 2019/790.

Bloomsbury Publishing Plc does not have any control over, or responsibility for,
any third-party websites referred to or in this book. All internet addresses given
in this book were correct at the time of going to press. The author and publisher
regret any inconvenience caused if addresses have changed or sites have ceased
to exist, but can accept no responsibility for any such changes.

A catalogue record for this book is available from the British Library.

Library of Congress Cataloging-in-Publication Data
Names: Saler, Robert C., author.
Title: The last true rebellion : "Death to the world" and apocalyptic
theological aesthetics / Robert Cady Saler.
Description: [New York] : [T&T Clark], [2024] |
Includes bibliographical references and index.
Identifiers: LCCN 2023049309 (print) | LCCN 2023049310 (ebook) |
ISBN 9780567704450 (hardback) | ISBN 9780567704498 (paperback) |
ISBN 9780567704443 (pdf) | ISBN 9780567704481 (epub)
Subjects: LCSH: Church work with youth–Orthodox Eastern Church. | Church work with
youth–United States. | Death to the world. | Christianity and culture–United States.
Classification: LCC BX342.6 .S25 2024 (print) | LCC BX342.6 (ebook) |
DDC 259/.23–dc23/eng/20240117
LC record available at https://lccn.loc.gov/2023049309
LC ebook record available at https://lccn.loc.gov/2023049310

ISBN:	HB:	978-0-5677-0445-0
	PB:	978-0-5677-0449-8
	ePDF:	978-0-5677-0444-3
	eBook:	978-0-5677-0448-1

Series: T&T Clark Explorations at the Crossroads of Theology and Aesthetics

Typeset by Integra Software Services Pvt. Ltd.

For product safety related questions contact productsafety@bloomsbury.com.

To find out more about our authors and books visit www.bloomsbury.com
and sign up for our newsletters.

"The generation of youth, today with the 'counter-cultures' of outcasts, metal-heads, death-metalheads, punks, skins, crusts, hard-core kids, skaters, gangsters, ghetto youth, mods, scenesters, stoners, junkies, etc. comprise this generation in search of identity, Generation X.

Through all these different movements there is one element that ties them all together. There is one common cry; there is one message that they all preach: Nihilism. As time moves on the confusion increases and the machine gains speed, working harder and faster. The youth of today can't help but be burned and scarred for life by this machine. There is no one to tell us that the fire burns; thus we must learn the hard way and hope that we don't die in the process."

–"Our Origins," *Death to the World*

*To all those standing in basement churches and basement venues,
keeping the faith that rebellion is still possible, this book is dedicated.*

CONTENTS

List of Figures	x
Acknowledgments	xi
INTRODUCTION: MARKETPLACE AND IDENTITY	1
Chapter 1 "MONKS ARE THE TRUE PUNKS:" JUSTIN MARLER AND THE BEGINNING OF THE MOVEMENT	25
Chapter 2 REACHING THE LOST GENERATION: THE ZINE BEGINS	41
Chapter 3 REVIVAL AND INFLUENCE	61
Chapter 4 WHOSE AUTHORITY TO FIGHT?	77
Chapter 5 THEOLOGICAL POTENTIAL(S)	97
CONCLUSION	113
Bibliography	120
Index	127

FIGURES

0.1	Inaugural issue of *Death to the World*. All images from the Death to the World zine and website courtesy Fr. John Valadez	8
0.2	Sample page from the zine *Death to the World*	9
0.3	Image of T-shirt sold on www.deathtotheworld.com	10
2.1	Image of St. Febronia, *Death to the World*	53
4.1	"Immunity." Image from Death to the World Instagram	90
4.2	"Banned Not Essential." Image from Death to the World Instagram	91
4.3	"Scream Destroy Riot." Image from Death to the World Instagram	93
5.1	"Orthodoxy or Death" T-shirt from Death to the World	103

ACKNOWLEDGMENTS

This book has been a multi-year journey that has taken me deep into my own past (coming from a punk rock background mingled with religion myself) and, more happily, into fascinating dialogue with a number of individuals whose lives have intersected with the various trajectories inaugurated by Death to the World. I began the research as a cautious, not uncritical, but sincere fan of the zine, the fashion, and its aesthetic reach, and I conclude it in the same place; however, the insights shared with me by others along the way have enriched that standing to a degree that I could not have anticipated.

First and foremost, I thank Justin Marler and Fr. John Valadez for their insights, corrections, and generous spirit along the way. Thanks are due as well to Christian Grimm of Redemption Barber Shop (much recommended for anyone needing a haircut in Dallas!) and 13th Vigil, Kevin Clay, Fr. Turbo Qualls, Matt Stein, Ryan Timothy Laferney, Bishop Gerasim, Dcn. Michael Wilson, Eugene Smith, Matthew J. O'Brien, Bonnie Bailey, Owen Schumacher, Roy Palvadeu, Fr. Joel and Maria Reynolds Weir, Sarah Riccardi-Swartz, Thomas Gaulke, Sujit Thomas, Sarah Lynne Gershon, and others who shared their perspectives and experiences with Death to the World with me (and offered helpful suggestions on the manuscript) along the way. Indeed, good stories and insights were so abundant in the slow gestation of this project that I have likely forgotten some people, of whom I ask forgiveness and commend to God's memory.

Several of the topics addressed in Chapter 3 of this book (around contexts of Orthodoxy in the United States) were worked out in conversation at the Center for the Study of Religion and American Culture at Indiana University/Purdue University Indianapolis, where I have benefitted from being a fellow for the last several years. Thanks especially to Philip Goff, Ray Haberski, Andrew Whitehead, Brian Steensland, Joseph Tucker Edmonds, and Peter Thuesen for their ongoing insights and support.

My godparents Peter Bouteneff and Pat Bouteneff have been excellent guides into the vibrant but landmine-laden worlds of contemporary Orthodox theological scholarship, and I am grateful for their wise guidance in that as in so much else.

As always, the staff and proprietors of Two Toms Brewery in Indianapolis are to be thanked for putting up with a nerdy professor in the corner booth, eating tacos, and writing about the apocalypse while innocent patrons are trying to enjoy themselves. And the faculty and staff of Christian Theological Seminary in Indianapolis, where I am privileged to teach, are gratefully acknowledged for their willingness to believe me that my bouncing between monasteries and punk rock/metal shows constitutes ethnographic research worth doing; I hope the following pages repay that confidence.

Special thanks also to Jennifer Newsome Martin and the editors of this splendid series, not least for pushing me to be more theologically forthcoming than is sometimes my wont. And I am grateful for the editorial team at Bloomsbury/T&T Clark for their patient guidance.

As communal as authorship always is, at the end of the day it also requires an unnatural degree of "alone" time, and the invisible labor of families in particular supports that endeavor. I am blessed with a family that has supported both the time spent putting words on pages and my various adventures in immersion in both Orthodox and punk rock culture along the way. My parish family, St. John the Forerunner in Indianapolis, IN, is a haven for oddballs like me who find their countercultural pasts merging with the ancient practices of Orthodoxy, and much of that tone is set by Fr. Zechariah Trent, to whom and for whom I am grateful. My parents, Larry and Elizabeth Saler, have supported their son's scholarly adventures even when the attraction of the subject matter has required a bit more explanation than normal, and that is a gift. And of course to Elise Erikson Barrett (who deserves most of the credit for anything intelligent/intelligible in the following pages when it comes especially to the life of the church and ministry), and to our crew: Elliot, Margaret, Erikson, Nora, and Cole. If apocalypse involves unveiling what is real and speaking truth about it, then family life is a daily apocalypse, and this book and my life are all the better for it.

INTRODUCTION: MARKETPLACE AND IDENTITY

WE CALL YOU TO JOIN US IN A TRUE REVOLUTION, the last true rebellion this failing world has ever known. You see, dear reader, we—likewise born into chaos, likewise gasping in a life of asphyxiation, likewise dirtied from our foolish actions—can attest to an urgent, life-and-death realization: Standing on the threshold of the authentic life requires alertness and the evasion of a predatory world that aims to draw you into its entangling and poisonous affairs. The authentic life requires one not to put to death the world outside oneself; the authentic life requires one to put to death the world inside oneself. All the world's hypnotizing idols must be toppled and shattered; all its deceptions must be exposed and rejected; all its protective masks—declared by some to be for your protection—must be ripped off and thrown away. In this process and only by this process does one encounter Truth, for Truth is not an abstraction, a philosophy, or an idea but a Person Whom one begins to know through action, contemplation, and transfiguration.

–Editors, *Death to the World*[1]

"We print in black and white because we want to form eyes to see color in the world." These words were spoken to me by Father John Valadez, a soft-spoken, heavily tattooed Eastern Orthodox priest in the Antiochian Orthodox jurisdiction, as we sat in a small pub in Lompoc, California, whose small-town feel belies both the military base and federal prison nearby, as well as its location less than an hour from the heart of Los Angeles. The occasion for the meal (and my journey to Lompoc) was to engage Fr. John about his leadership of the zine and website, *Death to the World*.

The notion of ascetic focus for aesthetic gain—that is, the disciplining of the senses and the body in order to perceive truth and beauty in the world in new ways—is one that an Orthodox priest might reasonably be expected to endorse. Orthodox theologian Timothy Patitsas has recently argued, with particular reference to the classic philosophical triad of transcendentals (common especially

---

1. "2020 Vision: From Blindness to Sight in the Age of Collapse," *Death to the World*, no. 27 (January 8, 2021), https://deathtotheworld.com/articles/2020-vision-from-blindness-to-sight-in-the-age-of-collapse/.

in Platonic and Neo-Platonic currents) of Truth, Goodness, and Beauty, that a properly Orthodox conception of ethics (as increasingly attested by classical and emerging voices in other disciplines) should not conceive of its task as beginning with truth (rationalism) or goodness (moralism), but with beauty. Patitsas correlates a progression of Beauty –> Goodness –> Truth with other theological and ethical triads familiar to Orthodox theology: chastity –> empathy –> humility, for instance. More directly, Patitsas links beauty primarily to eros for Christ in such a way that this desiring love becomes the ground for agape, and he goes further to name beauty in theophanic terms.

> The way of Orthodoxy, the way of "right Glory," is to begin by giving glory to God's Theophany (the beautiful) and then to practice the Good glimpsed within that Theophany. Through this eros which unfolds into agape, we participate in the True, and thus we become true ... Outside the Orthodox Church, Ethics is done backwards, moving from the True to the Good, and it is often done only part-way, never managing or bothering to reach the Beautiful. This is all right for certain purposes, especially in a secular society where reason is the only thing we all recognize in common. But when this truth-first approach occupies all of Ethics, it renders Ethics largely powerless to move and thus heal the soul. That which does not stir the soul in dynamic movement towards its telos cannot heal the soul.[2]

Beauty itself is oftentimes overwhelming and theophanic (disclosive of the divine); however, for Patitsas as well as other aesthetic theological thinkers, this beauty cannot be accessed even as excess without (somewhat paradoxically) a sort of ascetic discipline that focuses on the good through spiritual practices of right attention, prayer, and behavior in keeping with God's goodness. That is, excessive divine beauty is perceived most generatively and effectively through rigorous— even ascetic—focus.[3] This need for focus and attendant disciplining of attention is brought out well by Mark McInroy, who argues (in dialogue with one of the canonical figures of theo-aesthetics, Hans Urs von Balthasar) that, while beauty carries its own force and that force draws its energy from the divine, those seeking the divine in the form of beautiful objects (e.g., art or music) have the concomitant

---

2. Timothy George Patitsas, *The Ethics of Beauty* (Boston: St. Nicholas Press, 2022), 192.

3. C. A. Tsakiridou has argued that "beauty" as a theo-aesthetic mediating category is more typical of the Christian West than the East, with the latter preferring to focus more on the ways in which aesthetic objects such as icons manifest the divine "energies." While this possibility is interesting, both Tsakiridou and Patitsas ultimately are interested in how apprehension of the divine in aesthetic objects shapes us as humans and as believers, and so my inquiry will be concerned with the same. Cf. Tsakiridou, *Icons in Time, Persons in Eternity: Orthodox Theology and the Aesthetics of the Christian Image* (London: Routledge, 2013).

responsibility to prepare themselves for this engagement through disciplines sensory and spiritual.⁴

So too with Valadez's invocation of a black-and-white palette. What he was articulating was a philosophy (and theology) of transformation—from counterculture to ecclesial culture, from nihilism to truth. This theology, for almost thirty years, has been embodied in a material print culture that has extended now to clothing, digital engagement, and in-person communities, all under the rubric of Death to the World.

The book that follows is no less interested than the theologians already named in the ways in which beauty mediates the divine and reveals some degree of theological truth in ways that form and perhaps heal; however, given the phenomenon that Death to the World represents, our key interest will be in how this theological formation is mediated at collective as well as individual levels. What is a theo-aesthetic movement, and how can theology help us study it? Conversely, what can a movement—even a contested and at times problematic one—teach us about aesthetics and theology?

If one were to ask a contemporary Eastern Orthodox Christian in the United States what "death to the world" is, those who know of it will likely give a historical answer: *Death to the World* was a zine in the mid-1990s that, somewhat improbably given its subject matter, made significant waves in the fertile punk/metal scenes emerging in that period. A fair portion of those same Orthodox might also know that *Death to the World* was revived in the early 2000s, both as a zine (print and online) and, significantly, as a merchandise line drawing heavily upon the aesthetics of punk and metal T-shirts, pints, patches, flags, and other purchasable items.

But even Orthodox (and Orthodox-adjacent social media consumers) who are only vaguely aware of Death to the World's origins as a zine will likely be able to conjure a specific set of images, or at least aesthetic signals, upon hearing "death to the world": black-and-white images of particularly severe looking monks, skulls, iconography centered on martyrdom, and other "dark" or somber motifs. Theologically, they may also call to mind a certain pantheon of saints or blessed figures favored by the movement, such as Fr. Seraphim Rose or Saint Paisios of the Holy Mountain. Or, they may have noticed the hashtag #deathtotheworld appended to social media content that emphasizes the contrast between genuine Orthodoxy

---

4. "On this model, one perceives spiritually in the first instance not by having a set of faculties implanted within us from beyond ourselves (as Balthasar claims); instead, a great deal of spiritual perception occurs when occluding habits of looking are exposed and undone." Mark McInroy, "Spiritual Perception and Beauty: On Looking and Letting Appear," in Frederick D. Aquino and Paul Gavrilyuk (eds.), *Perceiving Things Divine: Towards a Constructive Account of Spiritual Perception* (Oxford: Oxford University Press, 2022), 213. Cf. also the articles in Elizabeth T. Groppe (ed.), *Seeing with the Eyes of the Heart: Cultivating a Sacramental Imagination in an Age of Pornography* (Washington, DC: Catholic University of America Press, 2020).

(or genuineness period) and ostensibly hollow or deceitful features of modern life, up to and including full-on polemics about vaccines, New World Order, and other conspiracy theory tropes. That said, the hashtag may also be appended to a particularly beautiful or salient insight about spiritual improvement, or "unseen warfare" between the self and ego, characteristic of the best of the Orthodox spiritual tradition. In line with Fr. John's words, and (as we shall see) in accordance with much of the punk and metal traditions from which the movement derives its aesthetic frameworks and energy, the core impulses behind Death to the World stem from positive content—self-control, attunement to God's will, spiritual maturity—as well as attacks upon modernity; however, knowing where the one stops and the other begins requires some parsing, including questioning whether the distinction finally holds.

Why Death to the World?

This book seeks to contextualize Death to the World within several overlapping spheres of inquiry concerning Eastern Orthodoxy in the United States. The project is best thought of as a case study in theological aesthetics in the sense that it seeks to demonstrate how a relatively small but powerfully influential phenomenon within US Eastern Orthodoxy sits at the nexus of a variety of larger questions, including: the relationship between formal ecclesial and para-church structures, the role of the internet in modern religiosity, consumer structures and patterns as constitutive of piety, the role of antimodernist rhetoric in contemporary Orthodox identity, constructions of "Holy Rus," aesthetic interplay between Christian practice and "sonic cultures," and more. While a wealth of important scholarship addresses these questions on both macro and micro levels, in this book I hope to synthesize insights from all these frameworks to illustrate how a specific phenomenon within US Eastern Orthodoxy provides insight into how one particular mode of contemporary religious identity formation happens in and among the porous boundaries of church, the internet, the marketplace, punk rock culture, and politics. In other words, I want to make the claim that Death to the World is interesting both in its own right and as a window into US Orthodoxy itself. I also want to argue that it is fertile material for the project of constructive theological aesthetics.

My hope is that this book, in addition to being the first scholarly treatment of the Death to the World movement, will demonstrate how this movement can be helpfully understood within a broader context of antimodernist subcultures both within American Eastern Orthodoxy and within American culture more generally (e.g., punk rock, new religious movements, underground fashion). Understanding Death to the World as an instance of lived religion and aesthetic contestation that is constituted among other things by patterns of production and consumption that are laden with questions of identity, politics of religious purity, ambiguous relationships to capitalist and online commerce structures, and concerns the darker sides of subculture helps us to see how negotiations of uniquely American Eastern Orthodox identity must be attentive to these broader cultural strands in supple, interdisciplinary—and theologically rigorous—ways.

Death to the World: Its History, Aesthetics, Production, and Influence

The roots of Death to the World and its cognate movements began in the 1990s. Justin Marler, a guitarist who was famous for having played on the first album by seminal "stoner metal" band Sleep, left the group after becoming fascinated with Eastern Orthodox Christianity. He became a monk at St. Herman of Alaska monastery in Northern California, a monastery started in the mid-twentieth century by American monk Fr. Seraphim Rose, a deeply influential figure in both Russia and the United States for both his charismatic spirituality and his many published attacks upon what he saw as the "nihilism" of contemporary life, particularly its various subcultures and countercultures. Marler would later relocate to a remote anchor monastery in the wilderness of Alaska for a period of seven years, where he worked (among other places) at the monastery's publishing house. This publishing house itself had established a reputation during Rose's lifetime for publishing spiritually intense materials. And thus Marler's punk lifestyle would soon become material for another kind of art, that of outreach.

Marler, along with several fellow monks, became fascinated by the ways in which more extreme stories and images of Eastern Orthodox monastics both ancient and modern correlated with the aesthetics of rebellion promulgated by the punk rock and metal scenes of which he and a number of the monks had been a part.[5] Like Rose, he saw the philosophical underpinnings of the latter as essentially nihilistic; however, in the same way that his own story embodied a "from punk to monk" ethos that saw the rigorous asceticism and rejection of modernity that characterized monastic life as a completion of the trajectory begun in punk rock culture, he saw an opportunity to produce a resource that would showcase to participants in American punk cultures what Marler could come to call the "last true rebellion:" rejection of the world in a religious sense and not simply a (sub)cultural sense.[6] The gamble, simply put, was that Orthodoxy could succeed

---

5. Marler's biography has been chronicled in multiple places. Cf. *inter alia* Shiloh Coleman, "Justin Marler: Warring against Yourself," posted November 15, 2018, https://www.shilohcoleman.com/blog/2018-justinmarler; Deborah Sengupta Stith, "The Unbroken Circle," posted December 4, 2015, http://specials.mystatesman.com/austin-punk-monk/; Emily Brown, "Death to the World: The Last True Rebellion," posted December 21, 2016, https://theoutline.com/post/715/death-to-the-world?zd=1&zi=mr2c6ow6. I will cite further autobiographical pieces and interviews in Chapter 1.

6. As Marler stated, "There are so many parallels that it was a real natural transition … Though it seems awkward to an outsider's eyes, it was really natural. There are a lot of similarities between the punk lifestyle and the monk lifestyle. Poverty, sleeping on floors,

in rebellion where punk had failed. He (and the movement) took the name Death to the World from a quote from seventh-century ascetic St. Isaac the Syrian which became the magazine's banner epigraph:

> "The world" is the general name for all the passions. When we wish to call the passions by a common name, we call them the world. But when we wish to distinguish them by their special names, we call them passions. The passions are the following: love of riches, desire for possessions, bodily pleasure from which comes sexual passion, love of honor which gives rise to envy, lust for power, arrogance and pride of position, the craving to adorn oneself with luxurious clothes and vain ornaments, the itch for human glory which is a source of rancor and resentment, and physical fear. Where these passions cease to be active, there the world is dead …. Someone has said of the Saints that while alive they were dead; for though living in the flesh, they did not live for the flesh. See for which of these passions you are alive. Then you will know how far you are alive to the world, and how far you are dead to it.[7]

It's important to note, for those less familiar with Orthodox theological terminology, that in Orthodoxy the "passions" are not primarily affective states (although they can be), but rather any mode of attachment that prohibits spiritual progress and attunement to God's will; hence, "death to the passions" correlates with becoming more "alive" to God.

As we will have occasion to discuss throughout the book, this teaching encapsulates a generative theological tension at the heart of Death to the World: the "death to the world" in question refers to the formative process of becoming "as dead" from the world's perspective, not "let the world die" or "kill the world." A story about the Desert Father Macarius provides an example of this teaching in Orthodox tradition:

> A brother came to see Abba Macarius the Egyptian, and said to him, "Abba, give me a word, that I may be saved." So the old man said, "Go to the cemetery and abuse [insult] the dead." The brother went there, abused [insulted] them and threw stones at them; then he returned and told the old man about it. The latter said to him, "Didn't they say anything to you?" He replied, "No." The old man said, "Go back tomorrow and praise them." So the brother went away and praised them, calling them "Apostles, saints and righteous men." He

---

not caring about what you look like, externally being a misfit in society because you look different. And this is my own opinion, but I think there's a lot of searching happening in punk rockers in their lifestyle and their music. And it's the same thing with monks: We're searching and probing into life." Quoted in Mark Athitakis, "A Punk's Progress," *San Francisco Weekly*, December 7, 2000, https://www.sfweekly.com/music/riff-raff-146/.

7. Death to the World, "About: What Do We Mean by Death to the World?" accessed April 3, 2020, https://deathtotheworld.com/about/.

returned to the old man and said to him, "I have complimented them." And the old man said to him, "Did they not answer you?" The brother said no. The old man said to him, "You know how you insulted them and they did not reply, and how you praised them and they did not speak; so you too if you wish to be saved must do the same and become a dead man. Like the dead, take no account of either the scorn of men or their praises, and you can be saved."[8]

"Becoming dead to the world" then is not the same as blowing the world itself up. However, it is also the case that the explicit agonism of ascetic labor against one's passions and the implicit antagonism toward many of the social, political, and spiritual structures that comprise "the world" allow for slippage between the two modes, "kill the world in me" and "let the world die."

With the encouragement and collaboration of Marler's fellow monks, *Death to the World* began its life as a "zine," that is, a self-published and self-distributed magazine of images and text replicated largely by photocopier. Both in content and aesthetics, zines have been an important medium within alternative music, art, and political cultures in both the United States and Europe.[9] The content, which as we will see was heavily influenced by several key twentieth-century Orthodox thinkers such as Rose, drew repeated contrasts between the perceived nihilism of both contemporary "status quo" American life AND the pseudo-rebellions (punk, Western turns to Eastern spirituality, occultism, drugs, and other countercultural practices) against it, on the one hand, and the spiritual purity sought by Orthodox monastics on the other; however, and crucially, the philosophical contrast was overlaid with repeated demonstrations (implicit and explicit) of aesthetic similarities between punk/metal imagery (skulls, dark clothing, dirtiness, crucifixes, and other death-oriented visuals) and monastics (see Figure 0.1).[10]

This interplay between cohesion in aesthetics and strong disjunction in content permeates the various articles of the magazine, many of which detail particularly severe or gruesome instances of asceticism, martyrdom, Christian persecution, or vivid accounts of the results of "nihilistic" decadence (particularly dabbling in

---

8. Benedicta Ward (trans.), *The Sayings of the Desert Fathers: The Alphabetical Collection* (Kalamazoo, MI: Cistercian Publications, 1984), 132.

9. Cf. Stephen Duncombe, *Notes from Underground: Zines and the Politics of Alternative Culture*, 3rd edition (Portland: Microcosm Publishing, 2017).

10. It should be noted that many of the contemporary monastic images featured in *Death to the World* are taken from Eastern European and Russian contexts, which for a variety of reasons tend to be more ascetically severe and "dark" than, say, Greek monastic settings. This, too, is likely due to the influence of Rose, who was a priest with the Russian Orthodox Church Outside of Russia (ROCOR), a branch of US Eastern Orthodoxy generally more conservative and ascetically severe than its counterparts in the Orthodox Church in America (OCA), Greek Orthodox Church in America (GOA), or Antiochian Orthodox Church.

Figure 0.1 Inaugural issue of *Death to the World*. All images from the Death to the World zine and website courtesy Fr. John Valadez.

New Age/Occult practices, drug abuse, and self-harm).[11] Like Rose, the theology of much of Death to the World presumes a universe made up of contestation between forces on the side of God (angels, saints) and literal demons, in which the role of humanity is to strive ascetically to keep the faith of the saints and resist the forces of corruption.

Issues of the zine, as well as an increasingly large merchandise selection of T-shirts, stickers, patches, and other punk-friendly items, were distributed at various punk rock and metal events, first in California and then nationally. At its peak, over 50,000 total issues had circulated (partly since, by design, zines are meant to be independently reproduced and distributed diffusively rather than from a centralized location).

Marler left the monastery in 1999, and the zine ceased operation for a time after twelve issues. However, the zine had attracted the attention of a younger generation of converts, including Fr. John Valadez, who along with a number of friends in the Southern California punk scene made their way to the monastery and received the blessing of the monks to revive the magazine as a website and merchandise store (www.deathtotheworld.com) in 2006. Since that time, the equivalent of nearly sixteen more issues (print and digital) have been produced, along with dozens of T-shirt and merchandise designs. Many of the shirts deliberately

---

11. This was also the content of a book written and published by Marler at this time. See Justin Marler and Andrew Wermuth, *Youth of the Apocalypse and the Last True Rebellion* (Spruce Island, AK: St. Herman of Alaska, 1995).

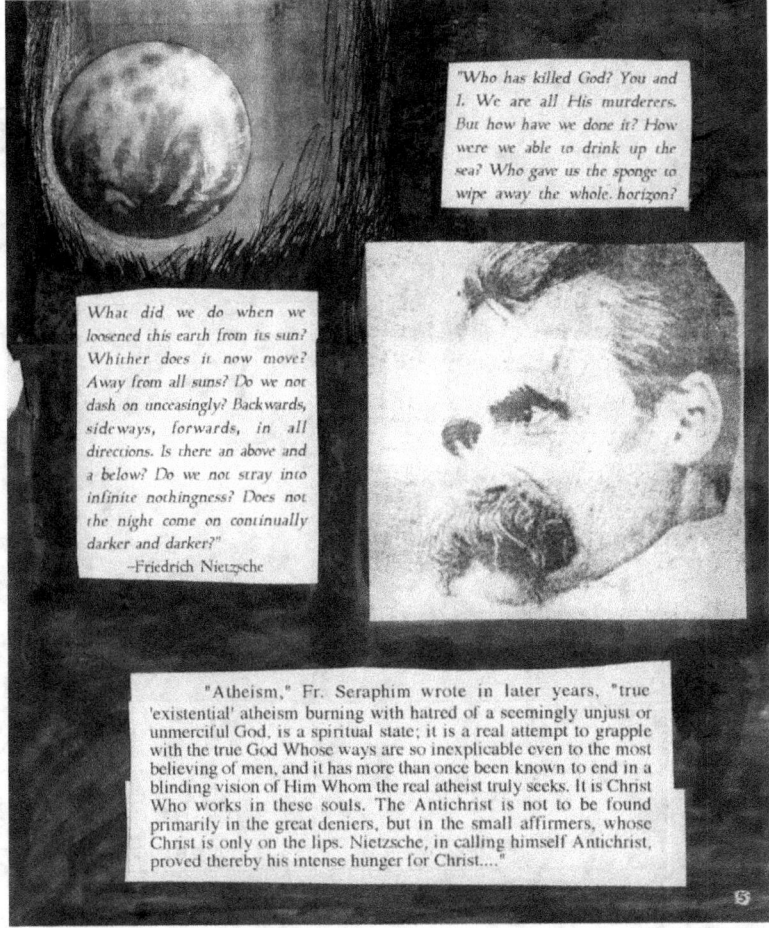

Figure 0.2 Sample page from the zine *Death to the World*.

invoke iconic metal and punk imagery, such as one featuring a Georgian monk performing baptisms with the caption "Baptize 'Em All" rendered in the same script as influential Metallica album *Kill 'Em All* (see Figure 0.3).

Valadez, having graduated from St. Vladimir's Orthodoxy seminary in New York, is now a priest in the Antiochian Orthodox Church in the United States and runs Death to the World from his parish in Lompoc, California. The site maintains an active social media presence as well (Facebook and Instagram especially, as well as the crowdfunded Patreon).

Marler, meanwhile, has continued in ministry initiatives which he understands to be cognate to Death to the World. His website "Unseen Warfare" bears a number of similarities to Death to the World in content, aesthetics, and merchandising

Figure 0.3 Image of T-shirt sold on www.deathtotheworld.com.

strategies (including T-shirt designs).[12] Other web-based independent clothing designers, including Orthodox Unlimited and 13th Vigil, have recently begun selling similarly designed T-shirts featuring both saints and martial imagery (which we will discuss below).[13]

12. www.unseenwarfare.net. The title comes from an influential sixteenth-century work of on ascetic theology by Lorenzo Scupoli. Cf. Theophan the Recluse and Nicodemus of the Holy Mountain (eds.), *Unseen Warfare: The Spiritual Combat and Path to Paradise of Lorenzo Scupoli* (New York: St. Vladimir's Seminary Press, 2007).

13. https://www.orthodoxunlimited.com/. It is worth noting at this point that the Byzantine war flag imagery featured on one of the "Orthodox Unlimited" shirts is often associated in contemporary times with Golden Dawn, a far-right Greek extremist party.

Because Death to the World encompasses an ongoing multi-decade swath of production (the magazine, shirts/clothing, website, etc.) as well as identifiable outreach efforts and a largely unified aesthetic, the book (following both Marler and Valadez) will refer to Death to the World as a "movement" within American Orthodoxy. To say something is a "movement" is a large claim. The choice of this term is not meant to strictly demarcate or to suggest that Death to the World's identity is uniformly understood and engaged across all relevant constituencies; rather, it is precisely to imply that key aspects of Death to the World have diffused and taken on lives/symbolic formations of their own within different facets of the Orthodox landscape. In other words, the very character of this "movement" is its relatively diffuse and porous boundaries that nonetheless point toward converging aesthetics and lived theological themes among a subset of American Orthodox. Death to the World is a zine, a fashion idea, a hashtag, an influence … and those that consume and engage with these products and influences are part of a trend worth studying.

To speak of a movement also raises the stakes for normative commentary, since social movements tend to outplace the strict intentions (and control) of their founders. Just like a text is shaped by the author's intention but will be interpreted by others in ways that exceed or perhaps even contradict authorial control, so too with social movements. In this book I will be making suggestions (hopefully grounded in close and charitable readings of Death to the World texts, images, and artifacts) for how the movement can evolve in ways that draw on its best features while mitigating some more problematic elements that have become associated with it; in so doing, I am appealing less to the founders and key authors associated with the zine itself and more to those, like me, who have a stake in Orthodoxy in the United States and in the movement's broader contributions to theology and our common life together.

Broader Contexts

In and of itself, Death to the World represents a relatively small phenomenon within an already modest minority within the US religious landscape (the United States contains only about 1 million Eastern Orthodox Christians, spread out over multiple distinct jurisdictions). That said, the purpose of the sort of focused analysis represented by this book is to demonstrate how small, often non-mainstream phenomena both exemplify and challenge larger trends and generalizations; in other words, intense scholarly focus upon local phenomena can demonstrate how multiple lines of inquiry intersect in concrete ways.

I want to assert from the outset that I view the turn to "lived" religion in many quarters of the contemporary academic study of religion as theologically valuable, not least for any inquiries into theological aesthetics. In the Christian narrative, God takes on a body, and traditions such as Eastern Orthodoxy that foreground the use of material images in worship and piety (such as icons) have, since the time of John of Damascus, asserted that this material is both blessed and a potential vehicle for the divine.

As we will see throughout the book, the case of Death to the World sits at the intersection of many key issues facing the study of lived Eastern Orthodox religion in the United States. These include:

1). *The interplay between marketplace consumption and religious practice.* Many of the assumptions and rhetoric around movements like Death to the World (by both proponents and detractors) assume a sort of purity of essentialized religious practice that is then brought into contact with market structures that threaten to disseminate only at the cost of dilution or pollution. Take, for instance, the following critique leveled at "the Orthodox zine that comically blends superficial Eastern Christian content with a hardcore-punk aesthetic":

> Started in 1994 in association with the then-schismatic St. Herman of Alaska Monastery in Platina, California, the zine's name, which in substance means detachment from "all earthly cares," is meant to appeal to angry, disenfranchised, and largely uneducated young men for whom "death to the world" means a nihilistic disdain for all humanity. More grotesque still is the zine's frequent use of skulls, graves, and other dark imagery not for the purposes of *memento mori*, but simply to look "cool." In many ways DTW's [*Death to the World*'s] cheap antics are similar to numerous anarcho-punk and crust bands using pictures of war crimes and other atrocities on their 7" sleeves, ostensibly to "send a message."
>
> ... Instead of being the subject of a positive news article, DTW ought to be derided by serious Orthodox Christians who have no interest in having their religion reduced to a fad. Those who find their way to Orthodoxy through DTW and other similar resources are likely to enter with a woefully incomplete and despicably inaccurate picture of what the Orthodox Church is. This is not what Orthodoxy needs, particularly in the United States where fervent religiosity often takes the shape of barking-mad hysterics.[14]

From this perspective, the supposed "real" Orthodoxy—represented by Schmemann and Meyendorff, both key figures in academic theological and ecclesial circles—is cheapened and discarded in favor of "pseudo" Orthodoxy as corrupted by marketplace opportunism. But it is worth noting that the same assumptions about essence, meanwhile, are operative even in the assumptions of Death to the World proponents who saw the outreach at punk festivals and such as a means of bringing potential adherents on a journey *out* of the subculture into the true faith.[15] In other words, both Death to the World's proponents and detractors

---

14. Gabriel Sanchez, "Death to Death to the World," *Opus Publicum*, December 30, 2016, http://opuspublicum.com/death-to-death-to-the-world/.

15. In personal correspondence with the author, both Justin Marler and John Valadez maintain that they no longer listen to punk rock music because it is too "worldly" and secular, focusing instead on gospel music (Marler) and liturgical music (Valadez).

tend to occupy the same essentialist frameworks about "true" religion and the marketplace.

This book takes a different tack. Influenced by theoretical frameworks that highlight the role of social structures in determining religion as an inherently pluralistic and contested enterprise (including theologically), this book will argue that it is unhelpful both analytically and concretely to posit some essentialized "real" Orthodox spirituality that subsequently engages (positively or negatively) the dynamics of neoliberal capitalism; rather, in historian Kathryn Lofton's terms, the very interplay between production and consumption—and the shifting demarcations of identity, worldview, and subjectivity that result— is itself constitutive of religious practice as such.[16] Moreover, this is no major problem theologically. I would argue that it is also theologically helpful in that this move works against the suspicion that secular study of theological movements will inevitably seek to "unveil," in Foucaldian fashion, the materialistic underpinnings of sincerely held theological beliefs in order to disclose some vaguely sinister power configurations. This book, in other words, will argue that to say that lived religion—in this case the American Orthodoxy practiced within Death to the World's circles—is constituted by complex negotiations of production and consumption, with concomitant implications for identity formation, is not a normative judgment either positively or negatively. It simply describes what is the case. Theological scholars and practitioners of Orthodoxy, to the extent that they are convinced of this, may theologize profitably as to how these configurations might produce life-giving results rather than destructive ones. I will try to make some normative theological claims along these lines throughout the book.

Another way of putting this is that Death to the World is an evocative test case for demonstrating that, empirically speaking, there is no hermetically sealed "real" Orthodoxy that is somehow advanced or corrupted by the sort of marketplace interventions that Death to the World and its cognate movements undertake; rather, for scholars of religion, understanding lived Orthodoxy as a mode of production and consumption is helpful particularly for the US context. This tracks with a move in American religious historical scholarship away from understanding the much-vaunted US "marketplace of religions" as somehow proposing strict (even if correlative) dichotomies between religious options and their commerce and toward seeing the boundaries between religious and market

---

16. Cf. especially Kathryn Lofton, *Consuming Religion* (Chicago: University of Chicago Press, 2017). Cf. also Michel de Certeau, *The Practice of Everyday Life*, 3rd edition, trans. Steven Rendall (Berkeley: University of California Press, 2011); Pierre Bourdieu, *The Field of Cultural Production*, trans. Randal Johnson (New York: Columbia University Press, 1993); Andrea Jain, *Selling Yoga: From Counterculture to Pop Culture* (Oxford: Oxford University Press, 2014).

practice as porous, shifting, and themselves constitutive of lived religious practice in the United States.[17]

This sort of work has the advantage, too, of serving as an intervention in vexed scholarly and practical questions concerning the identity of specifically "American" Eastern Orthodoxy. Orthodoxy's relatively brief history and relatively small numbers in the United States, exacerbated by the fact that many Orthodox communities in the United States are composed of immigrants and parishes under the jurisdiction of foreign patriarchates,[18] have made questions about what is "American" and "Orthodox" about "American Orthodoxy" particularly fraught.[19] Consistent with the argument above, I will not claim that the sort of identity-forming consumptive patterns characteristic of Death to the World somehow represents some "essence" either of American religiosity or its particularly Orthodox expressions; however, it is illustrative of multiple intersections of identity formation patterns whose contestation is perhaps uniquely characteristic of American Orthodox practice.

This rigorous anti-essentialism might seem needlessly provocative from a theological and ecclesial standpoint; historically and in the present, many theologians see the task of theology as adjudicating the extent to which a given thinker or thought is more or less in conformity with the "essence" of a

---

17. I follow here the articulation of this shift put forward by Jan Stievermann, Philip Goff, and Detlef Junker in the introduction to their volume *Religion and the Marketplace in the United States*: "While critics, academic and popular, might offer economic explanations for apparently peculiar religious practices, with further study, individual agency, actual practices, and the composition of religious groups have proved to be too complicated to be grasped by economic accounts alone. While theorists, as well as critical theologians, might define 'the religious' and 'the material' so as to be fundamentally opposed to each other, religious Americans then and now have usually been critical of certain kinds of economic practices while viewing others as being in harmony with or even important expressions of their faith." Jan Steiverman, Philip Goff, and Detlof Junker, "General Introduction," in Stievermann, Goff, and Junker (eds.), *Religion and the Marketplace in the United States* (Oxford: Oxford University Press, 2015), 11.

18. The highly anticipated but ultimately disappointing "Great Council" of Crete in 2016 was, among other things, convened to address the non-canonical status of the United States' "diaspora" Orthodox communities. Canonically, it is broadly understood that there should be one Orthodox jurisdiction in a given geographic region (e.g., the Russian Orthodox church, the Romanian Orthodox church, etc.). The United States has never had one unified patriarchate, which exacerbates tensions both globally (particularly between the Ecumenical Patriarch of Constantinople and the Moscow Patriarchate) and in the United States between such bodies as the OCA and the ROCOR.

19. Cf. David Bentley Hart, "Orthodoxy in America and America's Orthodoxies," lecture given at Fordham University in New York City, October 2, 2017, https://www.youtube.com/watch?v=WU3y_h47ByE.

given movement (e.g., "how Christian is this way of thinking?" or "is this really Orthodox?"). As we will see in what follows, the theological status of the prospect of "American Orthodoxy" (or, as some would have it, "Eastern Orthodoxy in America") is contested for historical and ecclesiological reasons that are specific to global Orthodoxy proper. So my argument is that to prematurely foreclose these tensions in an essentialist direction ("this is real Orthodoxy, this is not") is not only to risk lack of sociological historical precision, but also perhaps to undercut the work of the Holy Spirit in its ongoing shaping of the church in the American context. Such a future-oriented understanding of ecclesial reality may, at first glance, seem at odds with the self-understanding of many Orthodox Christians as possessing a fixed and unchanging theological legacy against novelty and heresy; however, as Orthodox theologian David Bentley Hart has recently argued (in contrast especially to John Henry Newman, but with application to any "fixed" understanding of the tradition as static), the dynamic and unfinished character of the church's tradition is vibrant precisely to the extent that it anticipates the horizon of the unknown future—what Hart, in terms germane to this book, terms "the apocalypse" of revelation's consummation.[20] Fidelity as preservation of indeterminacy undergirds the theological assumptions of my own work in this book as well.

2). *Punk rock culture and consumerism.* Ironically, those tracking controversies over Death to the World "selling out" pure Orthodoxy to punk rock consumerism may recognize key resonances with popular and academic discourse within the study of punk rock and counterculture movements in the United States more broadly. That is, the most "punk rock" thing about Death to the World might be the ambivalence of those within its orbit about its own existence as a commercial entity. Concerns about subversive counterculture movements being weakened or betrayed by taking on distribution/institution-building methods seen as endemic to mainstream culture are ubiquitous within all counterculture discourse (politics, art, new religious movements), and punk rock is no exception.

Specifically, attention to scholarly literature around debates within punk rock culture as regards identity, consumerism, and boundaries is germane to analysis of Death to the World in terms of "straight-edge" moralist movements within the culture,[21] wrestling's with white supremacist and nationalist appropriations of punk,[22] and commodification of an art form within the social structures ostensibly being critiqued.[23]

---

20. David Bentley Hart, *Tradition and Apocalypse: An Essay on the Future of Christian Belief* (Ada, MI: Baker, 2022).

21. Cf. Gabriel Kuhn, *Sober Living for the Revolution Hardcore Punk, Straight Edge, and Radical Politics* (Oakland, CA: PM Press, 2010).

22. Cf. Stephen Duncombe and Maxwell Tremblay (eds.), *White Riot: Punk Rock and the Politics of Race* (London: Verso, 2011).

23. For analogous cases drawn from classical music and experimental rock, respectively, see Jeffers Engelhart, "Arvo Pärt and the Idea of a Christian Europe: The

This book will layer scholarly analysis of the broader debates within the counltercultures (especially punk and metal) from which Death to the World specifically draws upon the specifically theological/religious debates within Orthodoxy into which Death to the World intervenes. Borrowing a term from seminal musicologist and communications theorist David Toop, the book will conceptualize both punk and Death to the World as "sonic cultures," that is, modes of listening and consumption that form fluid allegiances and patterns of identity.[24]

3). *Antimodernism, exoticism, and politics.* The modes of Eastern Orthodoxy from which Death to the World largely draws, following Rose, are fed by multiple streams; however, some features are ubiquitous. Among these are (1) a diagnosis of "nihilism" as the root philosophy behind modernity, and (2) a strongly grim and martial aesthetic tied to the resistance against modern nihilism. There are major debates within Orthodox studies now of how Orthodox subcultures, particularly online, relate to some darker antimodernist currents, including calls to violence. Here, too, layering this analysis onto the history of similar struggles within punk rock and extreme metal cultures will be instructive and ripe grounds for thinking theologically about the ongoing Christian imperative to resist such appropriations. Just as loving punk rock and metal means reckoning with some of the uglier subcurrents that have emerged within these subcultures at various times, so too appreciative engagement with Death to the World necessitates some hard wrestling with the ways in which its legacy, like that of all spiritually powerful sources, can be appropriated in potentially problematic directions.

4). *Orthodox contestations around laicization and technological platforming of monastic practice.* Orthodox theological scholars, clerics, and practitioners in various historical epochs and settings have wrestled with the question of how the strictures and patterns of monastic life (prized highly in Orthodoxy) relate to lay practice.[25] Because Death to the World is a product initially of a monastic setting, and the majority of its anecdotes and examples are of extreme ascetic practice on the part of monastic women and men, the movement stands as an interesting arteifact in ongoing negotiation between monastic ideals and lay practice. Other facets of Death to the World's implicit theologies can be examined within this framework; namely, if the monks are the most "hardcore" navigators of both social

---

Musical Effects and Affects of Post-Ideological Religion," in Jeffers Engelhardt and Philip V. Bohlman (eds.), *Resounding Transcendence: Transitions in Music, Religion, and Ritual* (Oxford: Oxford University Press, 2016), 214–32 and Robert Saler, *All These Things into Position: What Theology Can Learn from Radiohead* (Eugene, OR: Cascade, 2019), esp. Chapter 1.

24. Cf. David Toop, *Ocean of Sound: Aether Talk, Ambient Sound, and Imaginary Worlds* (New York: Serpents Tail Press, 2001).

25. Cf. inter alia Patrick Michelson, *Beyond the Monastery Walls: The Ascetic Revolution in Russian Orthodox Thought, 1814–1914* (Madison, WI: The University of Wisconsin Press, 2017).

and spiritual apocalypse, then what aspects of monastic piety and worldview are available to be transmitted and taken up within the mediums favored by the Death to the World movement?

Methodology and Goals

I should here signal my awareness that, at various points in the book, my method may seem more akin to secular "religious studies" (e.g., sociology or anthropology of religion) than theology proper. While I find historic contrasts between theology and religious studies to be overblown and not particularly helpful either on scholarly or theological fronts, it is worth being explicit and forthcoming about the fact that I understand thick, nuanced descriptions of the inner logic of theologically inflected cultural movements such as Death to the World to be both theologically valuable in its own right and as a necessary precursor to more normative theological work. As one whose academic training and current teaching work sit at the intersection of theology (as classically construed, more or less) and cultural theory, I am unable to think of one for very long without the other. And in the case of Death to the World, I will try to show that an entire disciplinary melting pot encompassing sociology, aesthetic theory, musicology, material religious studies, and media analysis is helpful as an analytic accompaniment to theology in drawing out questions of meaning related to the movement. Death to the World hinges theologically on the claim that God apocalyptically invades material history and becomes incarnate. Our analytic method should be no less incarnational in material and scope.

My hope is that the primary methodological innovation of this book will be to correlate the study of a phenomenon within American Orthodox religious history with parallel investigations into the history of debates around consumerism, identity, politics, and cultural formation within punk rock (particularly in American contexts). My contention is that Death to the World is profitably theorized as an episode within the history of American negotiations between punk rock culture and consumerism, just as those negotiations are ingredient to significant strands of American lived religion.

Much of the project involves engagement with texts. The ethnographic/qualitative elements of the research will come from ongoing engagement with the monks, priests, and publishers involved with Death to the World (including ongoing interviews with Marler and Valadez), but also field visits to Texas, St. Herman of Alaska monastery in Platina, CA, and St. Timothy Antiochian Orthodox Church in Lompoc, CA (from which the website, magazine, and store are currently run). While I have benefitted from a number of conversations with those involved directly and indirectly with Death to the World and while I will occasionally cite these discussions, for the most part I will draw upon published materials (especially interviews) with Marler, Valadez, et al. I do this both because the most salient points of our direct conversations, as it relates to the scope of this book, are captured well in these interviews and because highlighting publicly available data allows (and indeed, invites) readers to go to these sources themselves to decide if what I am taking from them is both accurate and germane. As the footnotes will indicate, much of this material is online and in video/podcast form, hours of which are available for consumption for those interested. Per my seminary's Institutional Review Board (IRB) policies, all direct verbal quotes to me where the speaker is identified have been cleared by that speaker for publication.

My primary training is as a theological scholar.[26] While this book will endeavor to give thick description of Death to the World and the overlapping circles of Orthodoxy identity issues in which it and cognate movements participate, it will also not shy away from the occasional constructive/normative comment about how Death to the World functions as an intervention in theological aesthetics more broadly. Constructive theology, in my understanding, can refer both to the task of making reasoned arguments for the superiority of certain construals of God (and then, by extension, of humanity, society, and ethics) over others, but also the analysis of cultural objects (explicitly religious or otherwise) on their own terms in order to draw out how attention to key themes in theological discourse past and present can helpfully illuminate both the objects/phenomena themselves and their implication for our common life together. I hope to do some of both.

As mentioned above, the Death to the World movement raises significant questions that benefit from normative ethical, political, and doctrinal analysis. Particularly in what I will argue is a contemporary turn toward more overtly political usage of Death to the World imagery, normative evaluation will play more of a role in my argument. However, my belief is that such engagement should proceed on the basis of the most richly nuanced understanding of Death to the World and its various contexts on their own terms as well as within the context of the most relevant strands of contemporary social, critical, and theological scholarship, and that is the task to which I am drawn and to which this book for the most part applies itself. Theologically speaking, too, I hope to demonstrate—if not foster in others—some appreciation for how Death to the World's characteristic aesthetic and theological themes can serve as provocative and generative interventions in contemporary theological aesthetics.

A few more words on what the book is not might be helpful. This book is not an exhaustive history or chronicle of the Death to the World movement. Such a book—which would of necessity encompass both written and oral histories, archival work, ethnography, and all of the requisite skills and techniques displayed by historians and social scientists—will, God willing, appear someday. However, as a theological scholar, I am not the one to write it, and to try to fit such comprehensive historical work alongside theological analysis in one book would be unwieldy at best and incongruous at worst. I will endeavor to give a robust

---

26. In many circles of Orthodoxy, the title "theologian" is an honorific given to certain saints and not an academic discipline per se; out of respect to the fact that many Death to the World adherents may hold that view, I will refrain from self-applying the title and describe instead the disciplinary location that orients this book.

description of both Death to the World and its context, and hopefully my work in both researching publicly available sources on Death to the World and my time immersing myself in conversation with those impacted by the movement will be apparent in both the prose and the footnotes of the work.

Having established what the book is not, then what do I hope that I have written? In crafting this inquiry, I have envisioned less a systematic theological argument unfolding step by step across chapters and more a narrative that highlights key moments in Death to the World's evolution while offering theological commentary. The aim is to highlight the depth, perils, and potentials of this phenomenon, both in the present and in potential futures. The reader may notice that, as academic monographs go, this one features a number of longer quotes; my aim there has been to give readers as much of an immersion into the prose stylings of both the zine itself and discourse around it as is feasible for this sort of book. If it's not a full-on florilegium, perhaps it may evoke something of the kind.

Reflexivity and authorial transparency are virtues both in the social sciences and in theology. With that in mind it should be stated from the outset that, as with my previous work on theology and music/music-adjacent phenomena (Radiohead fandom, Arvo Pärt, and other investigations into "sonic cultures"),[27] I write this book as a scholar who is also a fan. As may be evident in the pages to come, there is a particular fraughtness to some of the twists and turns within the variegated trajectories of Death to the World that make discernment between theologically promising aspects and problematic ones more high-stakes than, say, arguing the merits of a less beloved Radiohead album or a more experimental Pärt work. That said, both theologically and aesthetically, I find Death to the World's resolute insistent upon the centrality of the apocalyptic in spirituality, with an accompanying ethos that marries the ascetic with the "punk," to be—on the whole—a salutary and promising feature of the landscape of Orthodoxy in the contemporary world. Specifically, if nothing else, Death to the World keeps at the foreground of our theology the centrality of the apocalyptic, a mode of theologizing that (in Orthodoxy as well as in other traditions) is easily obscured under the conditions of modernity.

In short, I think the world and the church are better for having Death to the World in them. That is not to say that there are not areas where I find myself at odds with some strands of Death to the World's public presence (particularly as regards gender, sexuality, ecumenism, public health, and other contested topics); however, the book does proceed on the gambit that these more troubling aspects of Death to the World do not define it in such a way to rule out critical engagement and appreciation. While I am sure that my own background in the 1990s Midwestern punk scene (albeit as a fan and writer more than a musician proper) predisposes me toward some degree of recognition and fondness of Death to the World's project, it will be my task in these pages to make the case that the movement represents both

---

27. Cf. Saler, *All These Things into Position* and Peter Bouteneff, Jeffers Engelhardt, and Robert Saler (eds.), *Arvo Pärt: Sounding the Sacred* (New York: Fordham, 2020).

a theological achievement and a source of future potential, while also making clear where I see potential pitfalls in certain strands of the broader movement.

Working Definitions

It is useful at the outset of the book to clarify what I mean by "theological aesthetics" or "theo-aesthetics." Aesthetics, especially as a visual reality, are more than just how a certain thing looks. For the purposes of this book, I will define "aesthetics" as a complex (and sometimes multisensory) set of material significations, encapsulated in one or more material objects, that seek to evoke a recognizable web of meanings for those engaging them; likewise, in the case of specifically theological or theo-aesthetics, these meanings draw conceptual coherence (clear and recognizable meanings) and affective force (intensity of emotion) from the wellspring of lived religious traditions and discourses about God that inform the associations in play.

It is important to understand that any given symbol is indeed caught up in this broader web, and that correctly interpreting that symbol's aesthetic and theological significance at any given moment depends on taking context into account. Consider a cross, for instance. At a basic level it evokes the crucifixion and resurrection of Jesus Christ, a central event in the Christian narrative. But the interpretation of that event at a purely conceptual level, as well as the emotions that follow, varies even (and perhaps especially) among precisely those Christians who accord the symbol such importance. Does the cross primarily evoke sorrow over Christ's suffering? Or perhaps contrition over the human sin (personal, societal, cosmic) that, on some accounts, led to the requirement that Christ die to atone for those sins? Or even joy in the overcoming of sin and death through the cross? Perhaps some combination of all of these?[28]

And even beyond the conceptual level, a whole host of material aesthetic conditions come into play. Is the cross in question depicted in brutally realistic fashion, perhaps with a broken body wracked upon it? Or is it bejeweled, golden, worn as a fashion accessory in a manner that enhances the appearance of the one wearing it? Is it adorning a hospital sign in blue colors? Is it emblazoned across an assault rifle in the same manner that it once adorned the shields of Roman soldiers after Constantine's reign? Aesthetic setting as much as soteriology informs both the meaning and the emotional force attending the symbol.

A host of other questions are also implied in my working definition. For whom are the meanings and emotions of a given symbol or set of symbols evoked? Who are the implied and actual audiences? Like theology itself, and perhaps art itself, the variables attending interpretation are complex, multiple, and significant. But despite what is sometimes implied in caricatures of our (post)modern moment,

---

28. Cf. Khaled Anatolios, *Deification through the Cross: An Eastern Christian Theology of Salvation* (Grand Rapids, MI: Eerdmans, 2020) as well as Robert Saler, *Theologia Crucis* (Eugene, OR: Cascade, 2016).

interpretation is not an unbridled free-for-all. We can track both the originating impulses and finite responses to a given symbol's deployment in ways that allow for a correlation between a given theo-aesthetic strategy and that strategy's intended and actual effects. In other words, interpretation is multiple but not infinite, and some interpretations are more plausible than others. For instance, reactions to a photo of a modern saint holding his deceased mother's skull as a reminder of the inevitability of death (as in a recent *Death to the World* cover) may not be fully predictable or uniform (in fact they almost certainly will not be), but we do have enough history and data to understand to a certain degree how such reactions are likely to go, and what they might tell us about the worldview of the ones reacting.

What, then, is the Death to the World aesthetic? While it is risky to impose any one set of defining characteristics upon a movement without a clear set of boundaries (or boundary-keepers), as a working definition I have in mind the following general features. Not all of them are present in every instance of what I will refer to as Death to the World's aesthetic, but collectively they make up a sort of aesthetic orbit whose provenance within the movement is recognizable:

1. A relatively sparse and grim color palette, or stark red/black (evocative of classic heavy metal album covers and logos, and also the blood of martyrs).
2. A canon of particular saints and martyr-figures center-set on those noted either for ascetic severity or polemic against the contemporary world/modernity (e.g., Fr. Seraphim Rose and Saint Paisios of the Holy Mountain).
3. Invocation of rebellion against the false pretenses of the modern age (either in text or in parodic visual representation of modernity's excesses/evils).
4. *Memento mori* (remember death!) -esque representations of skulls, tortured bodies of martyrs, and other "somber" signifiers.
5. Textual or visual invocations of apocalyptic themes (either immanent in the sense of "unveiling" or teleological in the sense of the transitoriness of this life and the permanence of the next).
6. Consistent identification of nihilism as the core problem besetting modern delusions of progress.
7. Textual and visual representations of pretensions of human progress as actual or potential vehicles of the Antichrist.

In recent years especially, this list might be expanded to include such themes as the perniciousness of state intervention in church affairs (particularly around vaccine requirements and mandated church closures during the Covid-19 pandemic) and veneration of the Romanov family, especially Tsar Nicholas II, sometimes as an explicit contrast to the perceived growth of communist strands in the contemporary United States. Again, this is not an exhaustive list nor a litmus-style checklist; however, my hope is that the inquiry to come will flesh out the details and implications both of these individual components and their creative juxtaposition to give credence to my ascribing some degree of coherence (theological and visual) to the aesthetic.

But understood theologically, in the manner suggested by Patitsas above, aesthetics also form us toward a particular kind of perception of the divine and a corresponding ethic. In other words, from a theological perspective beauty is not just about enjoyment but about being shaped for discipleship, a life in God. Thus, particularly in the final chapters of this book, we will have a chance to sharpen the questions related to how these aesthetic features operate theologically, both in and of themselves and in concert with other influences.

Assertions

Ultimately, in what follows, I would like for the following core theses to remain constant, in the hope that they will provide both orientation for, and be validated by, the arguments to follow.

1. Death to the World as a phenomenon within Orthodoxy in particular and theological aesthetics more broadly parallels, and can thus be profitably illuminated by, similar issues within modern punk rock culture(s) around authority, consumerism, and the nature of rebellion in a world whose structures can so easily assimilate, repackage, and re-sell rebellion as status quo. In other words, punk can teach us about Death to the World and Death to the World can teach us about punk.
2. Death to the World is theologically interesting as a consistent outworking of an apocalyptic, otherworldly aesthetic that exists in necessary (and creative) tension with more immanent concerns: politics and culture wars especially. Indeed, as we shall see, while some might wish that Death to the World might remain more "otherworldly" than some of its current, more immanent trajectories might suggest, there are both historical and theological reasons why such a desire cannot be fulfilled all that simply. But the struggle to do right by otherworldliness by engaging the world in the right way is worth it, theologically and missionally.
3. The tensions over "perpetual rebellion" that are shared between punk and theology are inherent within "apocalyptic" (as both a theological and cultural genre) itself. That is, to be engaged in apocalyptic theology is to already be enmeshed in the sort of questions around rebellion, politics, and immanence/otherworldliness that Death to the World exemplifies. To the extent that is true, as a test case the movement can teach theologians something about the perils and promise of apocalyptic as a theological category/method.

My hope is that fans of the zine and the movement will recognize the portrait and find some value in the analysis that I offer. For the same reason, my suspicion is that those inclined to be suspicious of the movement will find ample evidence for their position in what follows as well. Ultimately, I am less interested in convincing readers to feel one way or another about Death to the World and more interested in making the case that it is a remarkably complex phenomenon worthy of attention and engagement.

While it is dangerous to presume too much about how readers might react to a book, my guess is that—for readers familiar with Death to the World—this text will be a sort of Rorschach test of how people feel about the movement. Those inclined to dislike or be suspicious of Death to the World will likely find in these pages plenty to reinforce their impressions, especially since I have tried to foreground as much text and testimony from the zine and its creators as possible. I hope that these readers find my arguments that Death to the World is interesting and worthy of study convincing, even if their impressions of the movements itself do not change. Meanwhile, my highlighting Death to the World content means that fans of Death to the World will hopefully enjoy the book, even though I will be asking them to believe me that, even when I am critical of some aspects of the movement, that criticism comes from a place of regard. And for readers completely unfamiliar with the Death to the World, hopefully the prospect of a phenomenon that sits at the intersection of two subcultures—punk/metal and US Orthodoxy—will be intriguing enough to make engaging the book's arguments worthwhile.

One further methodological note: the reader engaging the footnotes will note that, when I cite specific Death to the World online or zine articles, I sometimes give an author name and sometimes do not; this is because the zine alternates between naming authors of specific articles and leaving them anonymous. When a specific author is named, I will cite that author; when not, I will cite the article under the authorial heading "Death to the World." Likewise, when I am referring specifically to the zine, I will italicize the title *Death to the World*; when I am speaking of the broader movement, I will not.

Chapter 1

"MONKS ARE THE TRUE PUNKS:" JUSTIN MARLER AND THE BEGINNING OF THE MOVEMENT

The key to our restlessness, discontent, unbearable dejection and meaningless pleasure filled lives is clearly not found in doing what we want. It is found in exactly the opposite. It is found in a life lived in virtue and self-control. When we slay our desires, we slay our sorrow. When we train ourselves to practice virtue, we develop interior peace and contentment that is enduring. Love, chastity, humility, justice, kindness, goodness, faithfulness, gentleness, self-sacrifice and self-control are the cure to the human condition.

—Justin Marler[1]

Metal fans largely know the band Sleep as pioneers of so-called "stoner metal"—a subgenre of heavy metal music featuring extended, downtempo heavy guitar riffs that are crunchier than drone metal but crisper than sludge metal alongside lyrics extolling both marijuana use and the relatively fantastical/psychedelic images accompanying its use. In particular, Sleep's 2003 hour-plus extended track "Dopesmoker" is heralded as a high-water mark in the genre and has been the subject of accolades for over a decade. Prior to their refining this style though, the band began its recording career in significantly harsher sonic and lyrical territory. Their 1991 debut, *Volume 1*, is an abrasive affair both musically and thematically, with more frenetic guitar riffs and tracks titled "Stillborn," "The Suffering," "Anguish," and "Scourge"—more akin to doom metal than the band's more expansive, fantasy-laden later sounds. It is a brutal listen, sonically and lyrically.

Consider, for instance, the lyrics to the track "Stillborn":

Souls are siphoning
Spirit begins to drain—to drain

Feel the presence of obscurity
Nailed to the saw of reality

---

1. Justin Marler, "The Failure of Hedonism," *Death to the World*, Issue XXVII, accessed May 29, 2023, https://deathtotheworld.com/articles/the-failure-of-hedonism/.

Sad repressions
Deep impressions
In this womb
Remove and consume
Break control and remove this fetus.[2]

According to Justin Marler, the guitarist who played on *Volume 1*, the suffocating, misogynistic lyrical content of the album was reflective of his inner state while recording it.[3] A Chico, California native who, in his own words, described a "white trash" upbringing and a "miserable childhood," Marler's time in Sleep was marked by deep personal depression to the point of suicidal ideation and cutting. However, it was also a time in which seeds were being planted whose nurturing in the tensions between creativity and submission would soon bear a particular kind of fruit. This chapter, as well as the whole book, posits that Marler has and continues to function, if not as an Orthodox theological scholar, at the very least as a powerful public spiritual intellectual with success and influence in multiple public and ecclesial spheres.

Raised nominally evangelical Christian (in the Calvary Baptist tradition), Marler's childhood worldview was shaped less by religion per se (despite an early and lifelong belief in Jesus Christ as nurtured by his family) and more by his rejection of what he perceived to be the phoniness of modern life—a rejection given aesthetic and sonic shape by punk rock music and culture. While one could speculate that Marler's social location as the child of divorce, alcoholism, and family dysfunction might have predisposed him in this direction, it is equally valid to posit that an ability to sincerely occupy a countercultural milieu and to

---

2. Sleep, *Volume 1* (Tupelo Recording Company, 1991).

3. For the past decade, and increasingly even within the last year, Marler has given a number of podcast interviews telling his story before, during, and after Death to the World's founding. Details of the autobiographical sketch that I offer in this chapter are drawn from the following sources: Justin Marler, "Justin Marler: Warring against Yourself," interviewed by Shiloh Coleman, November 14, 2018, accessed at https://www.shilohcoleman.com/blog/2018-justinmarler; Deborah Sengupta Stith, "The Unbroken Circle," December 4, 2015, http://specials.mystatesman.com/austin-punk-monk/; Emily Brown, "Death to the World: The Last True Rebellion"; Justin Marler, "Justin Marler: From Metal to the Monastery," interviewed by Brother Augustine, May 27, 2022, accessed at https://www.youtube.com/watch?v=Ijc8DWem__Q; Justin Marler, "The Last True Rebellion with Justin Marler," interviewed by Buck Johnson, June 14, 2022, accessed at https://www.youtube.com/watch?v=7AkELO2V8kM; Justin Marler, "Youth of the Apocalypse with Justin Marler," interviewed by the Mad Ones, July 6, 2022, accessed at https://www.youtube.com/watch?v=OhGWSn2fA9E&t=5296s; Justin Marler, "Justin Marler of 'The Quick and the Dead,'" interviewed by Simon Head, *Apologue*, November 30, 2015, accessed at http://apologue.ca/epi-57-justin-marler-of-quick-and-the-dead/. I am also grateful to Marler for comments and clarifications in personal correspondence with me.

communicate its vitality to others has been—and remains—a lifelong talent of Marler's, from his time as a musician to his founding of Death to the World to his current ministry. As a very young child, he was asked by an older relative if he had given his life to Christ, and when it was explained to him what that meant, he did so—inaugurating a quest to see what impact such a commitment would have on his growing sense of his need to occupy counterculture rather than mainstream, worldly success narratives.

At age eighteen, Marler moved from Chico to the Bay Area, whose now-legendary 924 Gilman Street club was an epicenter of the particular strand of early 1990s punk that would soon become far more mainstream and commercially viable than its venerable predecessors (e.g., Sex Pistols, Naked Raygun, the Descendants, and so on) could have ever imagined for themselves.[4] This music would move from the relative margins of pre-internet musical outlets (MTV and contemporary commercial rock radio especially) to their center. Indeed, Marler lived in a warehouse in the Bay Area with members of Green Day, Operation Ivy, and Rancid, bands synonymous with punk's commercial turn. Here, too, we can pause and note that the scene Marler joined is one that, to a degree then unprecedented in the various strands of punk nascent since the 1970s, was suspended between the mandate toward authenticity and the lure, not only of potential stardom and financial rewards, but even more basically of the chance to make a genuine living as an artist and to be platformed in ways that allow that art to reach potential audiences that might resonate with it, all while being able to sustain oneself and one's loved ones apart from the perceived phoniness of the late capitalist rat race. Marler's career as an artist, writer, and public spiritual intellectual has consistently occupied and drawn energy from this tension—between absolute authenticity and sustainable compromise with the strictures of modernity. His is a life of truth-seeking amidst scenes always in danger of "selling out."

Punk as Lifestyle

We should pause and note here that there is no single agreed-upon definition of punk, musically or culturally. That said, people generally seem to know what it means when they hear the word. Musically, the language traces back to the fertile explosion of stripped-down rock styles in the 1970s that, partly in reaction to the perceived musical excesses of progressive rock and the lifestyle excesses of the stereotypical "rock star," offered a grittier, more aggressive, and often more sped up and musically simplified take on rock. Whereas, particularly in the New York Scene centered around the club CBGB's, the musical stylings of the Ramones, Television, Blondie, the Talking Heads, etc. were quite diverse, "punk" music quickly came to connote fast, aggressive, musically straightforward songcraft and

---

4. Cf. Kevin Mattson, *We're Not Here to Entertain: Punk Rock, Ronald Reagan, and the Real Culture War of 1980's America* (Oxford: Oxford University Press, 2020).

performance in the mode of the Sex Pistols (UK), the Ramones (US), and later such seminal bands as Minor Threat, the Circle Jerks, Black Flag, and so on. As Raymond A. Pattton puts it,

> When the Sex Pistols' "Anarchy in the U.K." hit the UK Top 40 the second week of December 1976, it sounded like nothing else on the radio ... Over the previous two decades, pop and rock had traded spontaneity and vitality for complexity and polish. For some, rock had become bloated and unattainable—music created by professionals for sophisticated listeners ... Then, in late 1976, punk arrived in the mainstream, courtesy of the Sex Pistols' "Anarchy in the U.K." on the radio. As though sensing his band was out of place at number forty-three on the weeks' hits list, Johnny Rotten laughs manically over a wall of overdriven guitar before snarling "I am an Antichrist/I am an anarchist," forcing the two phrases to rhyme against their will. The shock doubled for those who saw punk performed—cropped hair, straight pants, and a sneer instead of the flowing hair, bell-bottoms, and suave machismo that were standard for rock bands.[5]

Patton's invocation of fashion and visual aesthetics alongside the music is important; as Stacy Thompson points out, "there are several major genres of punk textuality: music (recorded and performed), style (especially clothing), the printed word (including fanzines, or 'zines'), cinema, and events (punk happenings apart from shows);" in Thompson's helpful phrase, "together, these texts make up the punk project."[6] One implication of this multi-textuality (quite relevant to consideration of Death to the World, a movement centered primarily in the printed word, images, and clothing) is that "over the history of punk, music has not always served as the textual form that best embodies the opposition at punk's core."[7] Hence, the materiality of the aesthetic beyond the music itself as being worthy of its own consideration alongside the music.

Many people hear "punk" and a 1980s-era image of mohawks and torn clothing immediately emerges. However, it is crucial to understand that when one studies the history of "the punk project," no one fashion or aesthetic style is dominant: the mohawks, spiked clothing, and leather of one generation give way to military stylings or even explicit clean-cut "normcore" of another, and the same is true for visual art as well.[8] What is almost always true is that punk culture reflects a contestation with the perceived mainstream, a struggle fraught with class, ethics, and (more often than one might guess) spirituality and meaning. When we talk, as

---

5. Raymond Patton, *Punk Crisis: The Global Punk Rock Revolution* (Oxford: Oxford University Press, 2018), 3.

6. Stacy Thompson, *Punk Productions: Unfinished Business* (Albany: SUNY Press, 2004), 3.

7. Ibid., 3.

8. Cf. David A. Ensminger, *Visual Vitriol: The Street Art and Subcultures of the Punk and Hardcore Generations* (Jackson: University Press of Mississippi, 2011).

we will in this book, of punk (and in some cases metal) as a "sonic culture," it is this intricate web of music, materiality, and cultural positioning that we have in mind.

All of this observation concerning material culture though is in service to analysis of the deeper aspects of punk culture that are most relevant as we consider Death to the World in theological perspective: punk as rebellion, but of a very particular sort. The core bands and ethos of the various punk rock movements in the United States, UK, and elsewhere did not (and do not) rebel against the status quo in the name of hedonism or desire to indulge pleasures condemned by more mainstream society—if anything, that sort of "rebellion" was characteristic of the mainstream "hard rock" that most punk bands despise both musically and ideologically. Instead, the core of punk's ethos—musically, lyrically, materially—is less about freedom from constraint per se and more about freedom from obedience to systems that seem irredeemably corrupt, arbitrary, and beholden to malign influences. Breaking free from bondage to these systems requires, in sonic cultures as in many religious ones, a complex web of philosophical and material signifiers, and aesthetics is ground zero for disciplined consumption and production of this web.

Marler's odyssey, then, as well as that of Death to the World as a whole, is best conceived as one particular and dynamic strand of this broader "punk project" as well as a spiritually intense conversation narrative.

Sleep, Suicide, and God

Soon after his move, Marler responded to an advertisement for a guitar player from the band that would become Sleep (then known by the one-word title AsbestosDeath). Even though Marler himself identified more with punk subculture than metal (and friction between those two subcultures has routinely been fraught), his time with Sleep was successful enough to earn the band a record deal (the aforementioned *Volume 1*), despite his own increasingly desperate suicidal ideations.[9] As Marler himself is quick to point out, it would be a mistake to draw overly sharp distinctions between his time enmeshed in the punk/metal scene and his growing spiritual yearnings. His entire career, like his life, has been God-haunted. Although he describes his evangelical Protestant theological formation as "theologically thin," his time with Sleep was saturated, not only by religious imagery proper, but also by a particular mix of religion and rebellion that

---

9. Indeed, one of the more confusing aspects of piecing together Marler's biography is that he generally self-identifies with the label "punk," even though his musical fame is tied to an unambiguously metal band. Post-Sleep musical projects by Marler have been more musically aligned with the punk genre (albeit tinged with metal and alt-rock influences). To the extent that other stylistic and aesthetic signifiers differ between the two genres, however, both punk and metal aesthetics are reflected in Marler's self-descriptions and among Death to the World fans.

bears some resonance with what was to come. For instance, as the band would rehearse at Marler's grandmother's house, they would read her Bible and search for evocative phrases to incorporate into their music. In Marler's view, despite the authentic darkness in the music, his pledge to Christ as a young child was still being outworked through his art. While heavy metal's appropriation of Christian and scriptural imagery is near-ubiquitous within the genre, the relative seriousness of Marler and his bandmates (several of whom, such as Al Cisneros of OM, would go on to form spiritually inquisitive metal bands of their own)[10] was evident. Religion and its questions—and the possibility of having those questions answered—were not a veneer or source of irony. It was a distant promise that lured the art toward deeper authenticity, even when that authenticity took the form of ugliness.

As a child of alcoholism, Marler was an early and consistent adherent of the "straight edge" punk ethos as popularized especially by Ian MacKaye of Minor Threat (and later Fugazi), who would later visit Marler at the monastery in Kodiak, Alaska. This ethos mandates a regiment of strict abstinence from drugs, alcohol, and promiscuous sex. While few straight edge artists and fans have rendered the movement's philosophy in explicitly religious terms, its underpinnings are deeply consonant with practices of asceticism across multiple spiritual traditions, including (and perhaps especially) Eastern Orthodox monasticism. This is so, not primarily because of the ascetic abstinence, but in the conceptualization of this asceticism as a formative influence promoting focus, clear-headedness, and readiness for struggle (spiritual, political, or otherwise).[11] It is also relevant that MacKaye, along with his Fugazi bandmates, has long served within the music industry as an ethical guiding light for bands determined not to "sell out" their artistic vision for corporate/monetary gain; all his musical projects refused significant financial rewards in order to tour and distribute music/merchandise in ways that remained true to their DIY ethic.

If, as I am arguing throughout this book, Death to the World can be conceived, not only as a phenomenon within US Eastern Orthodoxy but as an episode within the ever-unfolding ethos of punk rock in America, then we can clarify this point even further by specifying that Death to the World might be seen as a particularly theological fleshing out of the subjectivity and identity formation characteristic of the reflexive impulses of straight edge.[12] Straight edge is the aesthetic and spiritual

---

10. For example, OM's album covers feature unironic Orthodox iconography, as well as titles such as "God is Good."

11. Cf. *inter alia* Francis Stewart, *Punk Rock Is My Religion: Straight Edge Punk and "Religious" Identity* (New York: Routledge, 2017); Ross Haenfler, *Straight Edge: Hardcore Punk, Clean Living Youth, and Social Change* (New York: Rutgers, 2006); Kuhn, *Sober Living for the Revolution*.

12. Cf. Kennet Granholm, "Metal, the End of the World, and Radical Environmentalism: Ecological Apocalypse in the Lyrics of Earth Crisis," in Christopher Partridge (ed.), *Anthems of Apocalypse: Popular Music and Apocalyptic Thought* (Sheffield: Phoenix Press, 2012), 27–42.

godfather of Death to the World's melding of punk and monk, and it is another place where asceticism and the aesthetic merge. We will say more about this below.

Despite his band's success and his abstinence from the excesses of the stereotypical rock lifestyle, Marler's psychological state deteriorated during Sleep's ascendency; that said, even his despair took on religious overtones at times. In his telling:

> Grown up, I left Chico, and I moved down to the Bay Area for music. That was where Lookout Records and Gilman Street and this whole punk rock scene was emerging, and I wanted to be there and I was there, and I was really lucky to end up there, and ended up in a warehouse living with Green Day, and the members from Rancid, and a bunch of other bands, and it was before it all hit mainstream, and it was amazing, the camaraderie and the friendship and so on was amazing, but I was profoundly depressed and would cut myself with razor blades at nighttime and cry and beat the floor. And there was one time when I had the TV on just the static channel ... and I'd have the TV on and I'd be cutting myself and crying and I'd be like, man, I need to die. That's what I need. I need to die. And at the same time, I had this inculturation from Christianity in my white trash background, that kept on enduring through all of this and at one point I read the Book of Acts while I'm in the middle of this whole thing, and I read the Book of Acts and I was like, God, if your church actually exists, which I believed, this was the age of televangelists, and I just couldn't buy the idea that contemporary Christianity represented the Book of Acts. I prayed and I said, if your church exists, show me. Otherwise, kill me. And it was right at the time when I was recording the Sleep record that something happened. I snapped. And I snapped in a bad way, and I snapped in a good way. I snapped, and I decided that I needed to get out of the music scene, I needed to pull myself out of it, because it was only feeding it.[13]

This is in some respects a foreshadowing of Marler's later ecclesiology (or at least a retroactive recognition of it on his part), in that his prayers in his most desperate moments were not simply about God's existence or benevolence, but also about the desire for a concrete, embodied manifestation of a community and witness capable of conveying absolute truth. Specifically, Marler, thoroughly disenchanted with the ecclesial bodies of which he was aware, prayed to God to show him whether a true church existed or if instead all existing religion is a sham.

This is worth noting in part because it could have been otherwise; one could imagine, for instance, a situation in which Marler becomes convinced of the reality of Jesus Christ but, by natural inclination or acculturation, eschews any sort of formal, institutional (ecclesial) expression of this quest. The fact that Marler's impulses toward spiritual restlessness coincided—for him and for many that would

---

13. As quoted in Marler, "Justin Marler: Warring against Yourself," interviewed by Coleman.

later look to him for inspiration—with a concomitant quest for visible ecclesial community is an absolutely indispensable component of the Death to the World ethos. This is no perpetual rebellion against institutions per se; this is, rather, the quest for the right institution.

One can call to mind, as a sort of parallel, John Bunyan's titular character in the classic Christian spiritual writing *A Pilgrim's Progress*. At first blush, the protagonist's quest for religious truth may seem to be, not just a lonely one, but a structurally solitary one; church after church and fellow would-be Christian companions are all found wanting as the narrative moves along. However, at the core of this not-easily-satisfied discernment is the intense desire for real community, or, more specifically, community that partakes in truth together. The pilgrim engages his fellow travelers precisely because he is looking, not just for Christ, but for Christ's true church. With this goal in mind, the temporary failures of any given institution or fellow seeker are not fatal to the quest. So too with Marler. The search for truth and truth's institutional embodiment, the search for Christ and Christ's body, came together once the ecclesial reality of Orthodoxy became manifest in his life.

It's worth signaling here, in this regard, that some critics of Death to the World have viewed its appropriation of strategies more common in Protestant circles (e.g., religious merchandise, melding of popular and ecclesial aesthetics) as evidence that the phenomenon is more Protestant than Orthodox proper. Leaving aside our earlier comments about the undesirability of such essentialism, we can note at this point that the inextricability of the quest for Christ's truth and the quest for Christ's true church that we are describing in Marler, while certainly not unknown in Protestantism, took a specifically Orthodox shape very early on in the Death to the World movement. What is the original church of the apostles? What is the body that claims full truth and not simply a human interpretation of it? What is the body that has resisted novelty most effectively? These are the questions that drove Marler and continue to drive the movement for which his search remains an orienting narrative.

Finding the Church

On Marler's telling, it was in this spiritual and psychological state, in which he had already voluntarily left the Bay Area and moved back to Chico to clear his head, that he happened upon a small religious bookstore operated by an Eastern Orthodox nun. Marler, who by this point was also a burgeoning visual artist as well as a musician, stepped into the bookstore initially because he was intrigued by the iconography (even though, or perhaps because, his strictly Protestant upbringing forbade icons). Upon entering, and in a self-described confrontational spirit, he engaged the nun in theological debate on matters both aesthetic (the permissibility of icons) and ecclesial (the question of whether the church described in Acts is still an existing possibility).

1. Justin Marler and the Beginning of the Movement

Those familiar with scholarly literature on conversion in the North American context will recognize that this latter question is far from idiosyncratic; as D. Oliver Herbel has argued, the impulse toward "originalism" and continuity with the early church has been a strong impetus in Orthodox conversions on this continent for decades.[14] Where can the true church of Acts be found? In Marler's case, however, we can also see in this question a linkage characteristic of the nascent theological frame which continues to be operational in his work: the connection between truth and embodiment. Consistent in Marler, and very consonant with Eastern Orthodox theological epistemology, is the contention that truth is always and ultimately incarnated in specific embodiment—first and foremost in Christ, and by extension in Christ's church. This is a venerable patristic theme—think of Augustine's contention that the church is the *totus Christus*, the "total Christ" as embodied on earth[15]—and it provides evidence that, despite Marler's characteristically Western lack of Orthodoxy prior to his chance encounter with the nun, multiple aspects of his formation inclined him to view truth not as an abstract set of notions but as a formative power embodied in authoritative institutions, with those institutions themselves being at odds with mainstream cultural settings that cannot be similarly truth-bearing.

Continued engagement with the nun, and independent research on Orthodoxy (pre-Internet) at local bookstores, sent Marler on a religious quest with renewed intensity. He even took a pilgrimage to Jerusalem and lived there for a time, where this same confluence of historicity, materiality, and truth came into even sharper relief:

> I wanted to find God. I wanted to find Jesus. I wanted to be where he was. I was so hungry for Jesus Christ. And I didn't understand, at the time, my white trash background, the level of theology and theological understanding was really low in my family, so I didn't even know who he was. I knew that he'd existed and I knew that he was the son of God, but theologically I didn't understand that he was God incarnate. Like, I didn't understand that. And it was at that time that I learned about that from the nun. Jesus was God who became a man to redeem the human race. And that idea, the idea of Jesus dying on a cross and that he was the son of God was very simple, but understanding the incarnation, and then the crucifixion and then the resurrection, the whole thing blew my mind. And I wanted to just be where he was. So I made my way to the Sea of Galilee, and I walked around the sea of Galilee and I was just crying. I was walking around and just crying saying he walked here, somewhere, you know, he was here. And I happened to stumble upon this little hut, this stone hut, and it had a

---

14. D. Oliver Herbel, *Turning to Tradition: Converts and the Making of an American Orthodox Church* (Oxford: Oxford University Press, 2013).

15. Cf. Kimberly Baker, "Augustine's Doctrine of the Totus Christus: Reflecting on the Church as Sacrament of Unity," *Horizons: The Journal of the College Theological Society* 37, no. 1 (Spring, 2010): 7–24.

plaque that said something about Mary Magdalene. I don't, I think it was where he met her, or she wiped Jesus' feet with her hair or something, but all I could do was just fall down on the ground and be in awe, like truly in awe, And the whole time I was praying while I was there and asking God to like show me what to do and in the meantime I'm talking to Sleep and they're getting this record deal and asking me to come back and I was like so determined, like that was my dream as a kid, to have a record deal and to be in a band and play music and do that for a living, and it was so uninteresting to me.[16]

Upon returning to the United States, Marler drifted further from the music scene; in the meantime, intrigued by the nun's learning and lifestyle as well as his discovery of the *Philokalia* (a highly influential Orthodox collection of monastic texts), Marler inquired as to whether there were any male monasteries that he could visit. As fate or providence would have it, he was only an hour's drive from the relative mountain wilderness of Platina, CA (near Redding), where a monastery whose ethos and positioning within the Orthodox and US landscape would prove tremendously consequential for Marler and the zine he would found.

"It Is Later Than You Think"

St. Herman of Alaska Monastery in Platina, CA, was founded in the late 1960s by two monks: the Russian expatriate Herman Podmonshensky (who, as the later abbot of the monastery would later encourage Marler to found *Death to the World*) and Fr. Eugene "Seraphim" Rose, a former East Bay bohemian and talented Oriental linguist who, in a manner very akin to Marler, encountered a breaking point between his bohemian lifestyle and lifelong existential curiosity that eventuated in his discovering Eastern Orthodoxy, converting, and eventually becoming a monk. The influence of Rose's life, writings, and hagiography (he is considered by many to be a serious candidate for canonization) has yet to receive the full scholarly attention it deserves. For our purposes, we can say that no other figure (including Marler himself) is as influential on Death to the World's aesthetic and theological framework as is Rose.

While Rose is revered by US and Russian Orthodox especially for his personal sanctity and his insistence on the "otherworldly" character of Orthodox faith, many of his most famous writings find him with his gaze fixed squarely on his own cultural milieu. His body and heart were in his monastic cell and the liturgy; his mind was surveying the world outside. In his work, Rose constructs a declension narrative of Western civilization as a gradual slide, first into moral relativism, then nihilism, then (in his view) a coming totalitarian age of a dawning New World Order (which is the secular preparation for, and instrument of, the spiritual

---

16. As quoted in Marler, "Justin Marler: Warring against Yourself," interviewed by Coleman.

Antichrist). Characteristic of Rose's historical method is to interweave diagnoses of human prelest (spiritual delusion), conspiracy, millennialist ambition, and spiritual warfare into signature events of what he sees as the West's apostasy stemming from the East/West schism, the Renaissance, the Enlightenment, and so on.[17] Having told that story, he trains a similar mix of charges upon what he sees as deleterious currents of spirituality and culture in his own time, including the increasing popularity of "Eastern" religions in the West, the "charismatic revival" in churches, Christian acceptance of theories of evolution, and nascent transhumanist currents. What is crucial to understand about this catalogue of ills, from Rose's perspective, is that it is teleological and indeed relentlessly apocalyptic: each current of presumed self-improvement of humanity or "new" spiritual gesture is another step toward the coming reign of the Antichrist as seeded by nihilistic, posthuman theologies.[18] History is moving in a direction, and that direction is toward redemption via cataclysm.

---

17. For an intriguing recent historical argument that these Renaissance and Enlightenment currents, too, were undergirded by an apocalyptic theological eschatology, see John Jeffries Martin, *A Beautiful Ending: The Apocalyptic Imagination and the Making of the Modern World* (New Haven, CT: Yale, 2022).

18. "I will repeat something I said in the introductory lecture that the reason we are doing this is not just to have a view of what is true and what is false and throw out everything which is false and keep everything which is true, because everything I'm going to be talking about is false. But it will be extremely important for us to understand why it is false and how it went away from the truth. If we understand that, we have some idea of what goes on in the world today, and what is the intellectual structure against which we must fight. Although, while saying that everything I'm going to talk about is false, I mean it's false from the strictly Orthodox point of view. There, the whole, of course, is relative compared with what happens in the world today. All of these movements we talk about—Thomas Aquinas to Medieval art, to European Renaissance art and so forth—they all are very much more valuable than anything that has been happening in the world today. Nonetheless, there is a whole underlying worldview which produced these things, and we can see how it was departing from Orthodoxy. The history of the West from the Schism of Rome is a logical and coherent whole, and the views which govern mankind today are a direct result of the views held in the thirteenth century. And now that the Western philosophy dominates the entire world, there is no other philosophy except the Orthodox Christian philosophy which has any strength to it, because all civilizations have been overwhelmed by the West, this means that what happened in the West in these last nine hundred years is the key to understanding what is happening in the whole world today." Note: Rose's Orthodox Survival Course has never been formally published but is widely available and cited online (and occasionally bound and distributed in paperback by various monasteries). Like many of Rose's works, they have also often been passed around as samizdat both during the time of the Soviet Union and today. Seraphim Rose, "The Orthodox Survival Course," unpublished work, accessed May 29, 2023, https://www.patristicfaith.com/orthodox-christianity/the-orthodox-survival-course-by-father-seraphim-rose/.

Rose's invocations of nihilism, with its attendant apocalyptic theologies concerning the antichrist, are by no means superficial or offhanded; indeed, chronicling the genealogy, trajectories, and projected telos of nihilism in the West was a signature preoccupation of his intellectual work even prior to his becoming a monk. A precocious devotee of Bay Area bohemianism and, in particular, that scene's appropriation of Zen Buddhism (then a relatively new and exoticized arrival to the West) via his teacher, Alan Watts, Rose's embrace of Orthodoxy was, in a manner that prefigures Marler, both forward-looking and retrospective. While in his monastic (and eventually priestly) vocation and life he would dive deeply into the vast world of Eastern Orthodox spirituality (with more saints, writings, liturgies, ascetic traditions, and ecclesial particularities than anyone can hope to engage, much less master, in a lifetime), much of his writing as a monk prior to his death in 1982 was focused on what he took to be the nihilistic (and thus, by extension), demonic core of the cultural/subcultural milieus he had left behind.[19]

Rose's method in analyzing what he took to be nihilism's undergirding of much Western culture, philosophy, religion, and politics[20] was consistently genealogical and historical; in his major work on the subject (written just before founding the monastery), *Nihilism: The Root of the Revolution of the Modern Age*,[21] he traces the chronological development of explicitly nihilistic philosophy through its intensification via classic liberalism, then rationalism, vitalism, and finally the destructive impulses that he saw operative in both nascent postmodernism and totalitarianism. Throughout Rose's work, as has largely been the case with Death to the World, the three trajectories of nihilism (as philosophy), totalitarianism as expounded particularly in Leninist/Stalinist Marxism (as politics), and apocalyptic stirrings of the ascendency of the Antichrist (as theology) are intertwined and mutually reinforcing. As he commenced the work of founding and overseeing St. Herman's, he continued and expanded this tripartite historical analysis in such works as *Orthodoxy and the Religion of the Future* (1975), which applied this analysis particularly to so-called New Age religious movements as well as "ecumenism,"[22] and even more so in his sweeping review of Western intellectual history post-schism in his highly influential "Orthodox Survival Course" (variations of which

---

19. Cf. Hieromonk Damascene, *Father Seraphim Rose: His Life and Works* (Platina, CA: St. Herman of Alaska Press, 2003).

20. Politically, Rose anticipates much of Death to the World's preoccupation with monarchy as a superior political arrangement to liberal democracy, with its attendant celebration of the Romanov resistance to communism (and veneration of Tsar Nicholas II in particular; see Chapter 3).

21. Seraphim Rose, *Nihilism: The Root of the Revolution of the Modern Age*, reprint edition (Platina, CA: St. Herman of Alaska Press, 2001).

22. Both in Rose and in subsequent Death to the World writings on the subject, it is not always clear whether the epithet "ecumenism" applies most directly to syncretistic blends of

are still being taught, often by figures with at least some connection to Death to the World such as Fr. Peter Heers).[23]

Unsurprisingly, but to a degree and in a manner worthy of comment, is the centrality of Friedrich Nietzsche to both Rose and Death to the World's account of nihilism. In particular, Nietzsche's famous image in *The Gay Science* of the so-called "madman in the marketplace" is evocative both of the theological backdrop to Rose's contention (channeling Dostoevsky) that "if there is no God, then all is permitted," and to the particular overtones of rebellion that Death to the World would later amplify, not least by quoting the passage early and often.

The passage begins with a madman carrying a lantern and continually crying out in the marketplace in search of God. The people who hear him are unbelievers though and they are bemused, wondering if he is lost or afraid. The madman's behavior elicits yells and laughter rather than the urgent concern it demands. The madman responds with accusations:

> The madman jumped into their midst and pierced them with his eyes. "Whither is God?" he cried; "I will tell you. We have killed him—you and I. All of us are his murderers. But how did we do this? How could we drink up the sea? Who gave us the sponge to wipe away the entire horizon? What were we doing when we unchained this earth from its sun? Whither is it moving now? Whither are we moving? Away from all suns? Are we not plunging continually? Backward, sideward, forward, in all directions? Is there still any up or down? … God is dead. God remains dead. And we have killed him.
>
> How shall we comfort ourselves, the murderers of all murderers? What was holiest and mightiest of all that the world has yet owned has bled to death under our knives: who will wipe this blood off us? What water is there for us to clean ourselves? What festivals of atonement, what sacred games shall we have to invent? Is not the greatness of this deed too great for us? Must we ourselves not become gods simply to appear worthy of it? There has never been a greater deed; and whoever is born after us—for the sake of this deed he will belong to a higher history than all history hitherto."[24]

Christian and non-Christian religions, or to dialogue between Orthodox and non-Orthodox Christian ecclesial bodies (as in, for example, so-called "branch theory" or World Council of Churches-level collaboration, or both). Explicit anti-ecumenism is somewhat muted in Death to the World publications proper but is heavily present in aesthetic movements inspired by it, such as Orthodox Unlimited and 13th Vigil.

23. The Orthodox Survival Courses held in person at St. Herman's prefigure a number of aspects of Death to the World, particularly since they were quite popular among "counterculture" youth in the 1970s, many of whom would camp out Woodstock-style at the monastery in order to attend. See Chapter 2.

24. Friedrich Nietzsche, *The Gay Science*, trans. Walter Kaufmann (New York: Vintage, 1974), 181–2.

The madman expects a response, but the crowd has grown quiet, staring with astonishment. He throws his lantern on the ground, shattering it and putting out the light. The madman proclaims:

> "I have come too early," he said then; "my time is not yet. This tremendous event is still on its way, still wandering; it has not yet reached the ears of men. Lightning and thunder require time; the light of the stars requires time; deeds, though done, still require time to be seen and heard. This deed is still more distant from them than most distant stars—and yet they have done it themselves."[25]

As a number of scholars have pointed out,[26] the theological conflict described in Nietzsche's parable here is not first and foremost between Christian/theistic believers and atheists; rather, the conflict is between, on the one hand, what Nietzsche saw as his era's refined, bourgeois unbelievers who cling to the anemic vestiges of liberal society and its values even after the metaphysical verities that ostensibly inspired and supported them have been evacuated and, on the other hand, the prophet who understands that this evacuation, this "death of God," has rendered all these morals vacuous and untenable.

In other words, foreshadowing Death to the World's tag line, for Rose what is at stake in Nietzsche is the nature of true rebellion. Rose could, and did, grudgingly acknowledge the superiority of Nietzsche's passionate philosophical atheism to cultured bourgeois unbelief (or even nominal belief that carries no passion or commitment). Rose had spent much of his young adulthood in a similar intense atheistic state. Like Marler, even his rebellions against religion were God-haunted. For Rose and for much of the movement(s) he has inspired, if the choice is between the passion of Nietzsche and the lukewarmness of bourgeoise belief (or even unbelief), then Rose resonates more with Nietzsche, even as he sees him too as the key figure of the philosophical and cultural nihilism that leads to disaster. This foreshadows one of the main tenets of Death to the World and also prefigures the spirit of punk rock that we have been describing: no compromises. Radical nihilism and radical belief are the only two honorable (and ultimately viable) alternatives.

If Death to the World and its cognate movements could be said to have a patron saint who is not (yet) a saint, then Fr. Seraphim Rose is the clear candidate. Both in his philosophy and in his person, he provides a template for the sort of restless, rebellious seeker who finds in Orthodoxy the only safe harbor against nihilism. It seems hardly coincidental, then, that it was in his monastery, St. Herman of Alaska, that Marler would take the next steps in his journey.[27]

---

25. Ibid.

26. Cf. for instance Merold Westphal, *Suspicion and Faith: The Religious Uses of Modern Atheism* (New York: Fordham University Press, 1993).

27. We should acknowledge here that St. Herman of Alaska monastery has, at various times in its history and still in some quarters, been a source of controversy around both

1. Justin Marler and the Beginning of the Movement

Into Silence

I was on a mission for the real deal, you know? And here's what happened. When I first walked up the road to the monastery, the monastery is in a remote area in northern California on a mountain with no electricity and a well, a pump well for water, when I walked up there, the first thing the monks always do is they take you into the church to pray. And he took us, me and my friend, into the church and he showed us the church, he showed us where the altar was, he briefly mentioned the concept of communion, which is a continuation from the Last Supper, which is a continuation of the Passover, which Jesus fulfilled. Like the whole thing, I was just mind blown. And then he took me into this lower part of the church and he opened up a box and he had a candle, and with this candle lit, he showed me these little bone fragments in the box, and one of the bone fragments said James, brother of the Lord, and another bone fragment said John the Baptist, and another fragment that was actually a piece of wood that said the True Cross. And I started bawling. I realized my prayer about the church from the apostles was completely fulfilled in that moment. Like I'm standing here next to, they call it relics, remnants of these people that started the whole thing and continued the whole thing. I was done. I was done.[28]

Marler, whose headlong dive into Orthodoxy amidst the ruins of his punk lifestyle had brought him to the point where he was ready to conclude that coming to the Orthodox church was the answer to his prayer that God would show him the true church of Acts, would now encounter of level of intensity to that fulfillment that he likely could not have anticipated. After an initial visit with a friend to the monastery, he fell in love, not only with the surroundings and liturgy, but with the lifestyle of the monks, whom he quickly identified as the "true punks" (a point that he repeatedly emphasizes in talking about the period in interviews). The man who had spent formative time essentially homeless, sleeping on floors in warehouses and clubs alongside fellow musicians, now encountered men who rarely bathed, wore the same clothes day after day, slept on wooden planks, and cared even less for material success than did punk musicians.

But they did so for a purpose beyond rebellion, and their discipline (while akin in some ways to that of the artists whose company formed Marler) was a striving not simply for "authenticity" but objective truth. Just as it would be an incorrect read of Death to the World to see it as a melding of punk and Orthodox

ecclesial politics and allegations of misconduct. To investigate those claims and tell those stories are beyond the scope of this book; our interest here is in how the monastery formed Death to the World and how its continued presence (including its ongoing elevation of Fr. Seraphim Rose) has meant that it still functions as a sort of geographic center to the movement as well as one of its unofficial "pilgrimage" sites.

28. As quoted in Marler, "Justin Marler: Warring against Yourself," interviewed by Coleman.

ethos without the latter transforming and replacing the former, so too it would be superficial to see Marler's linkage of punk artists and monks solely as a matter of similar lifestyles or even aesthetic ideals. What was at the core, he discovered, was a theological vision of truth, and a church that claimed to manifest that truth across the ages.

Marler was hooked. After a few weeks spent wrapping up his art gallery and musical affairs in Chico, he joined the monastery as a novice, and was shortly thereafter tonsured a monk. His erstwhile bandmates in Sleep, while sad to see him go, were supportive both out of care for his well-being and, to a great extent, out of respect for his spiritual intensity.

He remained at the monastery under intensely ascetic conditions, both at Platina itself and then, even more intensely, for four years in the remote Alaskan wilderness of Spruce Island. In interviews, when he is asked about the time, he emphasizes how the rhythms of labor, liturgy, and pervasive solitude brought him face to face with himself and his own damaged past regularly: "I felt like a garbage can."[29] In his view, his main—indeed, his only—job as a monk was to contribute to the life of the community under obedience while spending most of his physical, mental, and emotional energy working on healing his soul under the guidance of the Church's wisdom and his monastic superiors. However, these same superiors would soon have other plans, and thus the story continues.

---

29. As quoted in Marler, "Justin Marler: From Metal to the Monastery," interviewed by Brother Augustine.

Chapter 2

REACHING THE LOST GENERATION: THE ZINE BEGINS

Father Herman Podmeshensky, the abbot of St. Herman when Marler was there, had been Fr. Seraphim Rose's closest companion and colleague; thus, it is perhaps unsurprising that one of his spiritual preoccupations was reaching out to a culture that he too perceived as caught in the grips of the collective outworking of nihilism. In particular, he was troubled by media accounts of youth addiction, mental illness, self-harm, and suicide; however, as an elderly Russian émigré to America, he was hardly in a position to know what would be most effective for reaching youth with Orthodox content. The arrival of a young, heavily tattooed novice whose credentials in the punk and metal community remained strong despite the bewilderment that some in the scene felt at his decision to abandon music for monasticism, presented the right opportunity. From the time of the Desert Fathers until now, Orthodox monasticism has always been caught in a complex spiritual and material economy whereby therapeutic work on the soul on the part of monks has been tied in with the dissemination of wisdom from the monks to the world, and Marler was about to step into that ancient economy.

Abbot Herman asked Marler how effective connection with youth subcultures happens. Marler responded that the credibility of zines, self-published magazines reproducible outside of corporate media channels and their control, was important. Abbot Herman then suggested that Marler and some of his fellow younger monks with varying degrees of familiarity with the subculture scenes in the United States start such a zine, and then go to shows and other venues to distribute it.

Marler was resistant to the idea at first. "It was sort of a torture, actually. All I really wanted to do more than anything was just sit in the woods of the monastery, and focus and not travel, not publish anything. I just wanted to sit there."[1] However, whether because he was finally convinced it was an idea worth trying or more out of obedience to his superior (a non-negotiable feature of all monastic life), Marler agreed.

As noted above by Thompson, the zine form has long been a part of "punk textuality." Generally considered to have begun in the 1930s in the science fiction

---

1. Quoted in Athitakis, "A Punk's Progress."

community as a way for fans of the genre to share self-authored fiction and critical commentary about their favorite novels, by the 1970s zines were a fixture both in the music scene and in other sectors of counterculture: veganism, leftist politics, alternative lifestyles, comic books, and other commodifiable countercultures.[2] Especially since the founding of *Maximum Rocknroll* in 1982, zines—with their often intentionally amateurish yet artistically ragged layout and their DIY, non-corporate models for production, reproduction, and dissemination—were well positioned to become a privileged mode of communication in a genre like punk where DIY authenticity and disdain for corporate media were virtues. Indeed, such a tactile materiality of non-mainstream reproducibility (i.e., you can hold them in your hands and you can copy them without permission) has caused zines to retain a great deal of global attraction both as niche commodities and as authentic, independent media even after the advent of the digital age.[3] Fr. John Valadez, who would revive Death to the World in 2006, captures the appeal well:

> If one were to walk through the doors of a concert venue and into the wall of people clad in leather and dancing to a blaring punk band screaming about some social revolution, you might be handed a black and white rough photocopied magazine by a mohawked youth filled will all sorts of art, social commentary, interviews from bands, etc. This is a 'zine … The photocopier makes it all happen. There are no rules to it, it's just usually text and images cut out and glued together to make up a photocopied version of a magazine that's handed out at shows as a revolutionary manifesto. The beauty of it is that people are able to make copies of their copies, thus the zines get circulated over and over again.[4]

If the medium is the message, then zines were the perfect media for the moment. Reproducible, decentered, anti-corporate; if authenticity was essential to punk ethos, then zines were perfectly positioned to embody that authenticity in material form.

It's important to note that, in thinking about what a seemingly surreal juxtaposition of Orthodox content with a somewhat nontraditional medial form might look like, Marler had found himself in a fortuitous location: not only had his years of formation in the punk scene given him an experiential awareness of the effectiveness of zine aesthetics, but St. Herman monastery from its inception

---

2. Cf. Stephen, *Notes from Underground*.

3. Cf. Michael Audette-Longo, "'Feel the Noise:' The Promotional Allure of Punk Fanzines," in Paula Guerra and Pedro Quintela (eds.), *Punk, Fanzines, and DIY Cultures in a Global World: Fast, Furious, and Xerox* (London: Palgrave MacMillan, 2020), 125–42.

4. Quoted in Marina Crissman and John Valdez, "Death to the World: An Orthodox Punk Zine Revived and Revisited," interviewed by Geraldine Fagan and RTE, *Road to Emmaus: A Journal of Orthodox Faith and Culture* 47 (January 17, 2018): 28–9, https://static1.squarespace.com/static/5e78f10494c7b26bc99e2fd2/t/5e8e23c472407957667f3e67/1586373572976/47.DEATH_TO_THE_WORLD.pdf.

had featured an active publishing ministry centered on a magazine called *The Orthodox Word*. Founded by Rose even before his becoming a monk, and still published by the monastery today, *The Orthodox Word* mixed hagiographical accounts (with a special fondness, inherited by Death to the World, for Russian saints persecuted under communism), original writings by Rose and others on the nihilism of popular culture especially, and art in such a way that, while not specifically as counterculture-oriented as Death to the World, clearly served as a significant template both for Marler and his fellow monks in creating the zine and for the monastery in publishing it. One might say that, as a zine, *Death to the World* is akin to *The Orthodox Word*'s rebellious younger brother.

The monastery library also had a wealth of material from Rose, who at the time of Death to the World's founding was less famous in the United States despite being quite famous in Russia (where, in a manner poignantly reminiscent of zine culture, his writings were passed around as *samizdat*—banned material—by underground Christian channels under Soviet censorship). All of these factors came together to make *Death to the World* a plausible enterprise within the context of St. Herman.

With the blessing of older monks (including the later Hieromonk Damascene Christensen, Seraphim Rose's biographer and current abbot of the monastery, and Monk Gerasim, later abbot of the monastery and now bishop in the Orthodox Church in America), Marler and his colleagues scoured print materials within the monastery and nearby libraries for zine content.[5] The standard way of producing a zine, which they largely followed, is to cut out pieces of content (like a photo or a text block), arrange and past the pieces onto a page, and then Xerox the page before stapling it all together (the late great copy chain Kinko's is cemented in punk history as the venue in which the final magic would happen).

In selecting content, Marler was driven by the same confluence that had been so decisive in his own spiritual life: the self-harming, nihilistic pain of youth despair meeting the extremes of Orthodox practice in the forms of rigorous asceticism, spiritual warfare, and sometimes gruesome martyrdom that is a part of the church's history (and, in some contexts of persecution, its present). This is an important point for understanding the theo-aesthetics of Death to the World both then and now: while, as we have already discussed, its aesthetic tends to focus on particularly somber elements of Orthodox history and culture—e.g., monks holding skulls, martyrs being tortured, and combat with demons, all in a black and white or similarly stark color palette presentation—none of this content in and of itself is particularly bizarre within the broader tapestry of church history. Visitors to monasteries across the world will regularly encounter the skulls of previous residents ("my future roommates," as some monks enjoy pointing out)

---

5. Bonnie Bailey, a friend of Marler's and later a nun at the monastery's sister convent, was also involved in the early inspiration for the zine; cf. David Boone, "Punkocalypse: Case Study of an Apocalyptic Youth Movement in Modern Times," unpublished article, accessed May 27, 2023, https://www.academia.edu/19489349/Punkocalypse_Case_Study_of_an_Apocalyptic_Youth_Movement_in_Modern_Times.

prominently displayed, even in monastery refectories! And as part of a religious tradition that is famously unsentimental about death in the handling of bodies during funerals (where the body is generally on display in the parish for well over a day and, traditionally, undergoes as little embalming or modification as possible), it is arguably not fully congruent for Orthodox to bristle at macabre imagery.

Valadez, in describing the zines revival, would later refer to the dark subject matter and imagery as "bait on a hook." For generations of counterculture youth used to pain and darkness (and its attendant imagery), the darker imagery of the church has the potential to resonate in ways that sunnier more upbeat religious images cannot (because the latter are generally associated either with phoniness or unacceptably mainstream cultural aspirations and their Christian veneers).[6] But, on Valadez's analogy, once the "hook" has hooked the youth, the whole rest of the church's aesthetic and theological palette becomes available for a lifetime of immersion. We will have much more to say about this in the chapters ahead.

The Rebellion Begins

Issue #1 of *Death to the World*, printed in 1994, wasted no time in announcing its mission and grounding theologies. The cover—in an image later displayed on what is now a much sought-after T-shirt—features Elder Nikodemus, dressed in full schema monk robes and holding a skull. Inside, after the above-mentioned Isaac the Syrian quote on the spiritual meaning of "death to the world" (as death of the passions) and a statement that *"Death to the World* is a zine to inspire Truth-seeking and soul searching amidst the modern age of nihilism and despair, promoting the ancient principles of the last true rebellion: to be dead to this world and alive to the otherworld," the issue opens with a full manifesto penned under Marler's name, one that is worth quoting at length:

> The last true rebellion is Death to the World. To be crucified to the world and the world to us. With the seed of dissatisfaction deeply planted in the heart of today's society, rebellion has been a small key to unlock the doors of change. But the rebellion that the world has known is not the fullness of true rebellion. Since our times have come to a point where things can't get much worse, the few remaining lovers of truth must search deeper into themselves and deeper

---

6. As quoted in the Floridoxy podcast, "Father John Valadez and Death to the World," accessed May 27, 2023, https://www.youtube.com/watch?v=RwQIidC1US4. This mental image is, of course, reminiscent of a key early Christian atonement theory, favored more now in the East than the West, in which God redeems humanity by means of a trickster operation whereby, at Christ's death, hell swallows Jesus' body thinking that he is only human, and then is harrowed when it cannot hold Jesus' divinity. Cf. Darby Kathleen Ray, *Deceiving the Devil: Atonement, Abuse, and Ransom* (Cleveland, OH: The Pilgrim Press, 1988).

into the truth itself—but to get to this point a revolution must take place. A revolution in the hearts of these lovers of truth. A revolution that annihilates all earthly and worldly thinking and that nurtures a way of thinking that is not of this world. Because that which is of the flesh is of the flesh and that which is of the spirit is of the spirit.

There is a grave necessity for this internal revolution, for only by this can progress be made. For how can one help a world with festering wounds until one mends one's own wounds. After this spiritual surgery has taken place, true rebellion is an ideal that is attainable. In this age of confusion and destruction, the necessary distinction between good vs evil has been deathly confused. The result of this is nihilism. The philosophy of nothingness, that no ultimate truth exists. In nihilism, there is neither love or hatred, good or bad, life or death. The result of this is the soul destroying idea that even God does not exist.

The natural reaction to all of this is an internal rebellion of the soul, for the soul cannot deny its own existence. At this point an all-out unseen war is fully engaged. In the case of the lover of truth, the rebellion manifests itself externally in a rebellion against this corrupt world. This is good, but there are too many people who just stop at this point. Without searching any further, how can one expect to uncover the answers? True rebellion will stop at nothing in the fight for the good of the world, for the good of others, and for the good itself in whatever way it manifests itself. It is necessary to wage a revolution in the heart in order to conquer evil with good so as to have a rebellion in truth. This is the kind of rebellion that must take place or else it isn't rebellion at all.

There once was a counterculture with the sole purpose of rebelling against the world. This counterculture was wise in the sense that its philosophy was based on recognizing the corruption of the world. In this lies half of the truth. It represents more truth than the world would ever dare to acknowledge. But this counter-culture must not stop at this, but must seek unto death the ultimate in truth if it is to accomplish that which it first set out to do: to care for and tend the world's wounds.

This counterculture of Punx is something that a handful of truth seekers can easily identify with, for it is very clear that the world is coming to a close. To be a true punk is to have nothing to do with that element which kills, hurts and causes pain, but to cauterize wounds. To be in the world but not of the world.

In actuality the true ideals of punk have yet to be introduced to the Punx themselves, as does the fulness of their rebellion. These ideals and this philosophy are the world's best kept secret. A secret that has been in the souls of those few lovers of truth ever since the beginning of time. The philosophy of punk has been around for centuries in the hearts and souls of the true Punx ... The Monks.

Monks are those who for thousands of years have rebelled against the corruption of this world by severing all chains binding themselves to the world. They have fled this vain world to live in caves, in holes in the ground, and to dwell in the deserts. To eat maybe once a day or even once a week, to wear the same clothes until they completely fall apart, and to rarely sleep because the cause is more important than the pleasures of this world. In these deprivations and sufferings they would realize one thing: There is no real suffering at all than to not know God.

This is the last true rebellion: To forsake the world and to embrace God alone.[7]

This article by Marler contains, *in nuce*, the broad themes taken from Rose and advanced through what would become the Death to the World movement: spiritual roots of society's decline, the concomitant deleterious effects upon the mental health of youth, nihilism as both the telos and the grounding philosophy of the modern age, and the invocation of Orthodoxy (and, in particular, monastic asceticism) as the repository of both theological truth and true counterculture. These basic themes have remained unchanged in the decades since the article was first written.

It's worth noting, from a literary-critical as well as theological standpoint, the implicit legitimation that Marler's early years as a punk ascetic—sleeping on floors, voluntarily living in squalor, sacrificing material comfort in obedience to his ideals of art, truth, beauty, and counterculture—lent (and continue to confer upon) Death to the World's invocation of a particularly severe monasticism. This, in turn, helps us appreciate how Death to the World itself functions as a sort of brief in favor of the centrality of monasticism in the North American Orthodox imagination. To be sure, monasticism and its attendant modes of spirituality hold a critical place throughout virtually all Eastern Orthodox thought and practice; however, the continued promotion and aesthetic signifying of relentless monastic severity—alongside a theo-aesthetic that emphasizes the particularly grim aspects of some monastic practice, such as eating meals in rooms full of the skulls of deceased monks or sleeping in coffins—has been instrumental in establishing world-denying asceticism as a privileged mode of what it means, within the Death to the World imaginary, to be Orthodox at all. And it's equally important to see that the aesthetic strategy here operates as a certain visual and affective casting of monasticism that is quite distinct from many other available depictions of Orthodox monasticism (many of which emphasize ascetic struggle but often in the context of the beauty of monastic settings—sometimes austere, sometimes excessively lavish in their vibrancy and aesthetic palettes).

My point in emphasizing this is to suggest that the same modes of authorial legitimation that lends authority to Marler as well as Death to the World's depictions of monastic austerity may have—perhaps inadvertently, perhaps not—set a theo-aesthetic agenda for the movement that presents a somewhat constricted version of the range of Orthodox monastic spirituality. That is to say, not all Orthodox monks look and act like those in the pages of *Death to the World*. The relatively dark palette—aesthetically and theologically, as it were—is not the only "monastic" aesthetic available in the church's tradition. In and of itself this

---

7. Justin Marler, Introduction to *Death to the World* 1 (1994) accessed May 27, 2023, https://deathtotheworld.com/articles/death-to-the-world-issue-1/.

may not be problematic or even particularly noteworthy; however, when (as we will see in future chapters) this privileging of a particularly severe palette of anti-world options is combined with increasingly conspiratorial thinking around the gathering forces of a perceived Antichrist, the picture that emerges of Orthodox theology and practice runs the risk of becoming less robust, multifaceted, and self-critical than the tradition itself.

But we can reiterate too what we said in connection with Nietzsche and Rose above: we cannot underestimate the sheer power of how *Death to the World*, from its very inception, made youth desperate for a word of reality amidst their darkness feel seen, understood, and preached to. Evidence for this is abundant then and now; as we have seen and will see, consistent testimony from those engaging Death to the World from the start describe it in similar terms: a word of ancient truth in a sea of cheesy, phonily upbeat religion. An empathetic guide that, in a manner similar to an addiction support group, understands pain and self-harm from the inside. A voice of rebellion that offers the same critiques of contemporary brokenness that punk culture does, but with a path beyond perpetual rebellion into peace. Where some not used to the punk aesthetic might see a strange mutation of standard Orthodox rhetoric, many saw a familiar vibe pointing toward a totally unfamiliar possibility of connection and healing. As Rose himself argued, "When conversion takes place, the process of revelation occurs in a very simple way—a person is in need, he suffers, and then somehow the other world opens up. The more you are in suffering and difficulties and are 'desperate' for God, the more He is going to come to your aid, reveal Who He is and show you the way out ... "[8]

The remainder of the sixteen-page issue is a microcosm of the sort of content that the following twelve issues of the zine's initial run, from 1994 through 1998, would offer: an article by Monk Damascene on Rose and contemporary youth; an account of a recent twentieth-century martyr under Stalin; short quotes from more ancient ascetics and saints such as Augustine (who, in a manner following Rose but in contrast to many Orthodox, Death to the World tends to esteem and quote regularly) as well as more recognizably Orthodox figures such as St. Seraphim of Sarov; and poetry about the quest for truth, all laid out against a backdrop of somber art and photographs of monks. While issue 25 of the zine's revival would move the zine to full color, the same templates for content and style have more or less been in place since this first issue.

Which Apocalypse?

It is worth pausing the narrative at this point to consider the theological context of "apocalyptic" into which *Death to the World*, following the influence of Rose in particular, was stepping from its very first issue. Given how easily the term can slip

---

8. Seraphim Rose, *God's Revelation to the Human Heart*, 5th edition (Platina, CA: St. Herman of Alaska Monastery, 2007), 43.

into colloquialism (e.g., "the results of the midterm election were apocalyptic!"), and given how central the notion is to the theology of Death to the World from Marler forward, we should attempt to define the term with some historical and conceptual precision even as we recognize that, like most evocative notions, it operates in polysemic fashion within Death to the World and cognate Orthodox movements (as well as in other sectors of American Christianity, notably evangelicalism).[9]

As is commonly stated, in its core etymology the term "apocalypse" simply means "revelation" or "unveiling;" however, in the context of both Death to the World and the cultural/theological energies upon which it draws, a more robust eschatology is implied. From a historical/textual standpoint, we can follow John J. Collins' formal definition of apocalypse (including in its biblical dimensions) as "a genre of revelatory literature with a narrative framework, in which a revelation is mediated by an otherworldly being to a human recipient, disclosing a transcendental reality which is both temporal, insofar as it envisages eschatological salvation, and spatial insofar as it involves another, supernatural world."[10] While this definition has the virtue of being general enough to encompass much of the historic literature that has been classified "apocalyptic" in genre terms, from a theological standpoint some other implications are key. In particular, notions of crisis, danger, judgment, and the divine rupture of history that bring about salvation for believers and destruction for that which (and perhaps those) oppose them have all come to be connoted within the term. Bernard McGinn helpfully expands on Collins' definition by distinguishing apocalyptic eschatology from Christian eschatology (in this context, discourse about the end of history from a chronological and agential standpoint) more generally:

> Eschatology is any form of belief about the nature of history that interprets historical process in light of the final events (*ta eschata*). All Christian views of history are eschatological in this sense, whether or not they stress the approaching end and the sequence of events leading to it. Apocalyptic eschatology, however, goes a step further in emphasizing a deterministic view of history. In apocalyptic eschatology the last things are viewed in a triple pattern of crisis-judgment-reward, and their imminence can be discerned in the events of the present through the revealed message found in the sacred book.[11]

---

9. Cf. Matthew Avery Sutton, *American Apocalypse: A History of Modern Evangelicalism* (Cambridge, MA: Harvard, 2017).

10. John Collins (ed.), *Apocalypse: The Morphology of a Genre* (Missoula, MT: Scholars Press, 1979), 9. Elsewhere, Collins points out that the term "apocalyptic literature" was coined in 1832 by the New Testament scholar Friedrich Lücke in the context of an introduction to the book of Revelation. John Collins, "Apocalyptic Eschatology in the Ancient World," in Jerry L. Walls (ed.), *The Oxford Handbook of Eschatology* (Oxford: Oxford University Press, 2008), 40.

11. Bernard McGinn, *AntiChrist: Two Thousand Years of the Human Fascination with Evil* (New York: Columbia University Press, 2000).

McGinn's invocation of "judgment" here points toward an essential feature of "apocalyptic" in its Christian theological sense: the revelation of history's meaning and the interpretation of history in light of last things are not understood by believers to be simply informative, but rather formative. It is meant to influence behavior in the here and now, in anticipation of the last things. Apocalyptic worldviews, we might say, are meant to be operationalized in belief, ethics, and lifestyle.

The career of apocalyptic within contemporary Christian theology has been uneven; while New Testament scholar Ernst Käsemann famously claimed that "apocalyptic was the mother of all Christian theology" in 1969, that claim is largely remembered today for its seemingly counterfactual status when applied to the mainstream theology of his day.[12] For reasons related to skittishness around over-emphasis upon otherworldly eschatology in general (particularly in the wake of the Feuerbachian, Marxist, and Freudian critiques that such "otherworldly" promises were compensatory for earthly suffering and thus unhelpful for projects of articulating theology relevant to suffering in the here and now), as well as a more generalized "demythologizing" trend that tended to treat overly literal understandings of the end of history as unhelpfully mythological, strong emphasis upon apocalyptic literature largely migrated from mainstream academic theology to (then) more marginal evangelical or fundamentalist circles as the twentieth century progressed. We might note here that the fact that much modern mainline Protestant and Roman Catholic academic theology since the Enlightenment has largely been reluctant to fully engage the apocalyptic as a core topic is not at all tangential to the rise of Death to the World, since (as we will see below) particularly in the 2006 revival of the movement much of its energy came from young Christians disillusioned with what they saw as the overly "cheerful" and thus (in their minds) phony Christianity of the mainline Protestant churches.

David W. Congdon has argued forcefully that contemporary theology finds itself in a position where "the [theological] literature on apocalyptic has tended to obscure the ways in which this word has been associated with a variety of theological commitments, some of which are incompatible with each other."[13] He helpfully distinguishes two broad hermeneutical strands in the *status questionis* (among academic theologians at least) regarding apocalyptic. The first "is the view that the apocalyptic event is something literal, immanent, and directly observable"; as he goes on to explain, what is crucial about this first category is

---

12. Ernst Käsemann, "The Beginnings of Christian Theology," in William John Montague (trans.), *New Testament Questions of Today* (London: SCM, 1969), 102. Indeed, Käsemann discerned a weakening of this early Christian emphasis already in the canon of what became the New Testament itself.

13. David W. Congdon, "Eschatologizing Apocalyptic: An Assessment of the Present Conversation on Pauline Apocalyptic," in Joshua B. Davis and Douglas Harink (eds.), *Apocalyptic and the Future of Theology: With and beyond Louis J. Martyn* (Eugene, OR: Cascade, 2012), 127.

that "whether one understands the new age in supernatural or political terms, there is a *sequential ordering* of two objective world ages."[14] Congdon refers to this as "Apocalyptic [Option] A." The second or "Apocalyptic B" option "views the apocalyptic event as something nonliteral, transcendent, and indirectly or paradoxically present." For Apocalyptic B, "here the new age is understood in neither supernatural nor political terms, and there is a *simultaneity* of the two ages."[15] Apocalyptic A is more "classical" and rooted in ancient Jewish traditions. It is taken up in both the New Testament and contemporary political theologies that see the apocalyptic as a theological instrument in describing the fight for liberation against oppressive principalities and powers. Meanwhile, Apocalyptic B—in a mode of demythologization—is the more existential option of "unveiling" toward deeper truths and authenticity. As Congdon explains, "the event in all its living potency remains paradoxically present within each contingent situation without ever identifying itself with any single political mobilization or sociocultural mode of existence."[16]

The sort of apocalyptic that Rose put forth, which Marler and Death to the World took up, is, on the one hand, fairly clearly in Congdon's "A" category; it is hard to imagine a more literal take on the subject than Rose's without moving over to full-on Hal Lindsey/*Left Behind* territory. On the other hand, as we will see, the question of the immanentization of the content of apocalyptic (with its subsequent ascription of history-shaping influence, including malice, to all-too-human actors) is a tension present in Rose and also inherited by Death to the World, particularly in its encounters with conspiracy theory. The existentialism in this case is not so much a de-historicizing as it is a shaping toward perpetual vigilance, perpetual pattern-seeking, perpetual rebellion. Thus, slippage between the apocalypse as strictly historical and more broadly existential is a relevant factor even in as starkly deterministic a worldview as Death to the World's.

Again, in popular parlance "apocalyptic" draws from the somewhat ominous energy of "world-ending" even as much of its use in, say, cultural analysis also picks up on its world-shaping and world-remaking character.[17] For our purposes, though, we can identify the most salient aspects of apocalyptic as a theological worldview as encompassing a series of factors:

---

14. Ibid., 132. Congdon's emphasis.

15. Ibid. Congdon's emphasis.

16. Ibid., 133. A similarly helpful cartography of options for apocalyptic in contemporary theology, organized in part around the question of whether the apocalypse "unveils" concrete theological content or rather operates on a more existential/mystical level, is offered by Cyril O'Regan in his *Theology and the Spaces of Apocalyptic* (Milwaukee: Marquette University Press, 2009).

17. As in *inter alia* the essays in Partridge, *Anthems of Apocalypse* and Edward Whitelock and David Janssen, *Apocalypse Jukebox: The End of the World in American Popular Music* (Berkeley: Soft Skull, 2009).

1. *Deterministic yet with Contested Agency*: While the apocalyptic framework of Rose, Marler, and subsequent *Death to the World* authors is unambiguous in the framework of crisis-God's judgment-reward outlined by McGinn, the centrality of spiritual warfare in Rose (as prosecuted by both supernatural and human agents) means that the agential question of who is driving and shaping history at any given moment is complex and, quite literally, contested. This allows "apocalyptic" as utilized by Death to the World to function both as ascription to God's providence and as a demonology.
2. *Ethically Rigorous*: The black and white aesthetics of Death to the World is consonant with a similarly "black and white" worldview as regards the need to be uncompromising in obedience to the ethical demands of the coming judgment and coming Kingdom. As we have already seen, the notion of refusing compromise for the sake of going "all in" on one's convictions resonates deeply with the punk subcultures that comprise the backdrop to Death to the World's vision, and the sort of ethical clarity that (sometimes problematically) attends apocalyptically minded groups is unambiguously present in the movement. Lack of ambiguity does not, of course, always mean lack of complication.
3. *Perpetual Rebellion against the Principalities and Powers*: Given the previous two points, it makes sense that the notion of, as Death to the World often puts it, "rebelling against" or "resisting" the "spirit of the modern age" is a key motif throughout the movement. However, as we will be exploring throughout the rest of the book, it is also the case that this introduces the same sort of destabilizing questions into apocalyptic theology in this mode as are present in punk rock subcultures. Can rebellion really be perpetual? Is protest sustainable over the long term?

A significant generative tension within Death to the World comes from the fact that, while it ostensibly is an outreach movement designed to lead those lost within empty subculture existence into a space (the church) of rest, plenitude, and truth, its core aesthetic is one of ongoing rebellion against the principalities and powers of modernity in particular (ala Rose). Given how vociferously Death to the World has been utilized by those within Orthodoxy to continue exhortation to battle against these powers, it is clear that the war does not end once one has come home (i.e., to the church).

We will have much more to say about this tension throughout the book. For now, however, the point is that, to the extent that Death to the World is caught in contested territory as regards perpetual rebellion versus peace, that too is a parallel with (and perhaps direct result of) the apocalyptic theology that fuels its theo-aesthetic vision. And we will have occasion to continue to ask, to what extent does Death to the World's take on apocalyptic mediate its own kind of formative beauty?

From Zine to Movement

Following the Abbot's instructions, Marler and some fellow monks trekked to various shows and record shops in northern California, distributing the zine.

In an incident key to Death to the World lore, they also tried to take out a paid advertisement for the zine in the aforementioned holy grail of punk zines, *Maximum Rocknroll* (having previously been unsuccessful in submitting an article about Rose and counterculture to that zine, a rejection that may have contributed to the monks' motivation for starting their own). However, this ad too was rejected, which Marler now theorizes as emblematic of the failure of "liberalism" to have room for sincere religion in the (in this case literal) marketplace of ideas—a conclusion that, as we have seen, tracks well with Rose's genealogy of nihilism.[18]

Even without the early exposure that such advertisement might have yielded, though, response to the zine was swift. While its unusual style and content aroused predictable ire both from punks who had no use for religion intruding onto their scene (on the one hand) and less open-minded Orthodox Christians who had little sympathy for subculture-friendly presentation of the faith (on the other), more significant was the success that the zine had in reaching its intended target audience. Part of the beauty of zines that makes their impact tricky to assess is that their DIY reproducibility means that gauging the full extent of readership is impossible (although, as mentioned above, total estimates for circulation alone are plausibly in the tens of thousands); however, what became immediately clear from the flood of letters that the monastery began receiving from youth testifying to the effect of the zine and its content was having on them was that impact was indeed being made. Tale after tale of youth struggling with the very maladies theorized by Rose and experienced by Marler began pouring in: suicidal youth discovering the Jesus prayer, young people flirting with the occult reading the zine's injunctions on spiritual warfare, and passionate subculture participants being at first stunned, and then inspired, by the courage of the martyrs.

It is worth pausing again to highlight the literature and spiritual function of the more graphic accounts of martyrdom that have been a part of Death to the World's content from the beginning and remain so in the present. A particularly graphic, although not unrepresentative example, is this excerpt from the web zine of the account of the martyrdom of Saint Febronia under Diocletian in AD 305.

> Moved to wrath again, the persecutor ordered that four men stretch and bind the nun so that they could mercilessly beat her back. The pitiless men beat her for a long time, whilst others made a fire under her and sprinkled the fire with oil, causing her worse burns. Witnessing this atrocious punishment the crowd cried aloud, "Have compassion on the young woman!"
>
> On the contrary he ordered his men to increase the scourging and beating. When it was seen that the strips of her flesh fell to the ground and that she appeared dead, he commanded that she be cast to one side. Seeing her move he said aloud, "How did the first match seem to you, Fevronia?" Christ's martyr answered, "Know that in the first trial with Christ helping me, I not only remained unconquerable, but I regarded your tortures with contempt."

---

18. Eventually, *Maximum Rocknroll* would accept an advertisement.

The prosecutor then said, "Suspend her upon the wooden pole and lacerate her sides with iron claws; then burn her torn members to the bones." They tore at the saint so that her flesh fell to the ground and her blood streamed forth as a river. Later they brought fire and burned her entrails. Looking steadfastly up into heaven she said, "Come to my aid, O Lords, and do not abandon your servant."[19] (See Figure 2.1).

Figure 2.1 Image of St. Febronia, *Death to the World*.

19. "Saint Febronia: Beauty Bathed in Blood," *Death to the World*, July 10, 2014, https://deathtotheworld.com/articles/saint-febronia-beauty-bathed-in-blood/.

What to make of this as a piece within a contemporary zine/website?

The first thing to say is that, again, such visceral details are hardly absent from the most venerable hagiographical accounts of martyrdom that we have, as even a cursory reading of, say, the martyrdom of Perpetua reveals. Death to the World represents a particular mode of curating the church's stories, but it does not fabricate or embellish them. Second, by the time of *Death to the World*'s initial run, a fixture of punk culture was performance of bodily manipulation (and in some cases mutilation, most infamously in the performances of G.G. Allin who himself was the subject of a *Death to the World* article upon his death[20]). Again, much of Death to the World's authenticity in commenting on punk culture comes from its depth of familiarity with that culture's more niche elements, and this understanding of body manipulation for the sake of transcendence (however misguided apart from the church) is an example of just that resonance. And third, as we have seen, the outreach to suffering youth that was key to the motives for Death to the World had as its particular focus youth self-harm; thus, highlighting stories of saints and martyrs whose bodies underwent significant torture, but for righteous causes, seems to have been a particularly effective choice for resonating with the contexts into which the zine made its way.

Thus, Marler's publishing ministry quickly morphed into a national (and, as the zine spread abroad, where again Rose's reputation was already well-established, eventually international) listening and counseling ministry,[21] one that has continued today even after Marler's formal association with the monastery and the zine has ended.

In addition to the zine, Marler undertook two projects related to *Death to the World* during the midpoint of his monastic career. At the Abbot's encouragement, in 1995 he recorded an album of acoustic songs called *Lamentations* with lyrical content similar to the poetry featured in the zine and released it on cassette; he

---

20. "Two Deaths," *Death to the World*, March 11, 2013, https://deathtotheworld.com/articles/two-deaths/.

21. Per David Boone: "By 1996 the Death to the World mission, also colloquially referred to as the 'Youth of the Apocalypse' after Justin's newly-published book of the same name, was a bustling project. Hundreds of kids came out to the monastery to visit and many chose to take lifelong monastic vows and stay. Press runs of Death to the World exceeded a thousand per issue—fairly huge in zine-culture standards. A summer Missionary School was established at the Brotherhood's St. Paisios Abbey in Forestville, CA, where young pilgrims could study theology, liturgics, apologetics, hagiography, Church History, philosophy, and other subjects from an Eastern Orthodox perspective. A 'Youth of the Apocalypse Conference' was held in fall 1996 in order to brainstorm ways of 'reaching the lost' with the truth of Orthodoxy; in this case, the 'lost' were the kids on the fringes of society who were understandably cynical and embittered by the usual Christian panaceas of pie-in-the-sky and milquetoast Protestant 'salvation'. Cross-country mission trips to both secular and Christian music festivals were organized, Death to the World t-shirts were designed and silkscreened, and back issues of the zine were reprinted." Boone, *Punkocalypse*, 7.

then toured coffee shops both in the United States and Europe to play the album and promote the zine. In addition, in the same year he and fellow monk Andrew Wermuth published a book, *Youth of the Apocalypse and the Last True Rebellion*, now a sought-after collector's item,[22] but then widely distributed, which contains a mix of hagiography, theology, and manifesto content similar to that of the zine. In it, the authors' ongoing concern with the links between nihilism and youth despair and suicide, all against the backdrop of antimodern apocalypticism, is apparent:

> This generation of youth, which could very well be the last generation, is shackled in despair ... because they see all too well that this broken world is coming to an end. And no one has told them the truth that in the apocalypse God will wipe every tear from their eyes. But they have been taught by violence that this eternal truth is "relative"
>
> ... After spending our childhood in such a cold prison, it's no wonder that our youth seek death. When there is no answer to the question, "Why?" the only freedom seems to be suicide. When there is no truth in a world of falsehood; when there is no love in a world of violence and hate; when there is no God in a faithless world, it's no wonder that in every room, on every street, in every city, the weeping of the young can be heard. That is why youthful rebellion is justified.[23]

The authors go on to identify, Rose-style, nihilism as the philosophical culprit behind the despair born of relativism and assert that only the truth found in the church's witness across time can be the substance of true rebellion. *Youth of the Apocalypse* stands as a sort of catechism in miniature for the movement: despair, nihilism, Orthodoxy as witness across time, and martyrology form the itinerary and movement from soul damage to soul healing.

While both the zine and the book understood pleasure-seeking as a stage along the way toward spiritual ruin, one thing that is remarkable about Marler and his colleagues' vision at this time was their unrelenting sense that the true fruits of loss of meaning are despair, self-harm, and suicide. This diagnosis stands in contrast to much of what would have been the rhetoric around punk in their day, that the lifestyle was unrelentingly hedonistic and unbridled in its rebellion against society primarily for the purpose of legitimating the exercise of prurient desires. Part of the appeal of *Death to the World* was how seriously it took the existential angst that, in Marler's view, fueled the punk rock lifestyle—the kids aren't alright, but not because they are undisciplined pleasure seekers. The kids, like Nietzsche, were more serious than the cultured despisers who mocked their pain while fulfilling the roles assigned to them by polite society. Nihilism was fatal, but the severity of the diagnosis came with a kind of gravitas that clearly resonated with many youth who encountered the zine.

---

22. Long out of print, copies of the 1995 edition now sell for hundreds of dollars on used book sites.

23. Marler and Wermuth, *Youth of the Apocalypse and the Last True Rebellion*.

Movement and Community

As Marler toured extensively, lecturing, performing, and promoting the zine and book, others inspired by the zine and its vision began creating outposts to embody the energy of the movement. Throughout the late 1990s and into the new millennium, in collaboration with the monastery, a series of Orthodox bookstores and coffee shops with variations on the "Punks and Monks" theme opened shop, concentrated especially on the West Coast and Alaska. Popular Orthodox author Frederica Mathewes-Green, in her book *At the Corner of East and Now* (a copy of which would later fall into the hands of Fr. John Valadez and serve as his initial clue as to the existence of Death to the World) described visiting such a shop called Not of This World (the title of the first edition of Monk Damascene's biography of Seraphim Rose) in Santa Rosa, California, and being impressed with Death to the World and Justin Marler's story. She also interviews the monks of St. Herman to hear from them their take on the zine and the broader movement being inspired.

> "These kids are sick of themselves," said Fr. Damascene, "and they feel out of place in this world. We try to open up to them the beauty of God's creation, and invite them to put to death 'the passions,' which is what we mean by 'the world.' God takes despair and turns it around to something positive. Selfish passions can then be redirected into love for God, as Mary Magdalene did. We talk about the idea of suffering, because that is what the kids feel most strongly. We show that there can be meaning in suffering."[24]

While most of these bookstores in this first wave have closed, as we will discuss in the next chapter a second wave (centered largely online) has emerged in connection with the zine's revival.

In addition to the formal businesses, a number of intentional living communities (some functioning as lay "sketes," or small monastic outposts) emerged, some of which predated Death to the World but all of which received energy from the fusion of youth counterculture and Orthodox spirituality for which St. Herman's was fast becoming a center. Blogger Matt Stein, whose background parallels Marler's in some respects, has written movingly about his time at Theophany Skete near St. Herman, close enough to the monastery to where he also developed a friendship with Marler:

---

24. Quoted in Frederica Mathewes Green, *At the Corner of East and Now: A Modern Life in Ancient Christian Orthodoxy* (Chesterton, IN: Ancient Faith Publishing, 1999), 40. In the same piece St. Herman monk Father Paisius, Marler's godfather, is quoted: "This subculture is raucous and deeply disturbed because of their own pain. It's demonic; they're living in hell, overdosing on drugs, or maybe going into a rage and killing someone. They see life as worthless. We want to show them an ideal that is worth their life. These are marginalized youth who are wounded, and Death to the World is meant to touch with a healing hand that wound."

This idea was conceived by punks from the Bay Area that had left that scene and became monastics in these monasteries. They were fusing exiled pre-Revolutionary Russian monastic spirituality with elements of punk subculture. They embraced a deeply apocalyptic worldview, considering their generation "youth of the apocalypse." Their aim wasn't to change the world. Rather they sought a transformation of heart. Through a common life, the cycle of services, study and honest work, they found a path towards this goal. Theophany Skete was a place where this transformation of heart could be nurtured and sustained. It was a refuge from the heartless, materialistic, modern world, the same world that punks were rebelling against.

None of this was apparent when I arrived. It wasn't until after I met Justin, the monk in charge of the Skete, that this aspect of the Skete started to emerge. He told me a little about his background in the Bay Area punk scene. I found out that he was one of the foundling members of the band named Sleep. This band had played shows with bands that I had listened to growing up. Justin had lived a semi-homeless life, squatting in abandoned buildings, in rough parts of town, sometimes feigning insanity in order to not be attacked. This life took a toll on him. So, he left it. Somehow he ended up as a monk in a monastery as austere as the squats that he formerly lived in.

Meeting Justin was a breath of fresh air. Before meeting him, it had been really hard to relate to the other monks. Except for Fr Herman (and a couple of others) the monks seemed distant and unapproachable. Justin was warm and open. He was my age and we shared some similar life experiences. I was not a punk then nor had I been one previously, but punk music and culture had profoundly influenced my life.[25]

When one travels to Orthodox parishes across the United States today, it is not uncommon for someone to reminisce that "we used to have some guys living together doing the Death to the World thing."

A signal contention of this book is that the Death to the World movement has been, and continues to be, the fountainhead for a movement within both the church and (in a different sense) US punk counterculture; as the above examples make clear, throughout the 1990s during the zine's initial run, this movement became multifaceted and multi-platformed.

Back to the World

Marler has been reticent to comment extensively on his decision to leave the monastery in 1999, and for the sake of our inquiry here we can certainly respect that and not speculate overmuch. His public comments have made clear that he

---

25. Matt Stein, "Worlds Colliding," *These Buried Sparks*, January 22, 2022, accessed May 27, 2023, https://theseburiedsparks.substack.com/p/worlds-colliding.

eventually found the two enterprises of touring extensively while working on his own soul healing in relative solitude increasingly incompatible. More positively, he has also emphasized in interviews (and in conversation with the author) that a major part of his motivation was to take the insights and lessons that he learned from his time in the monastery and to apply and disseminate them in the crucible of modern life, from which he was almost totally cut off in the monastery. His ministry in the last two decades, in the context of raising a family and working various lay professions, has certainly born fruit in this regard; as stated at the beginning of this chapter, I contend that Marler has a subterranean but significant presence within US Orthodoxy still as a lay theologian and spiritual leader.

As was perhaps natural, shortly after returning to lay life he resumed his musical activities. Although in his music in the early 2000s he seemed uninterested in marketing himself as a "Christian rock" artist, his musical work (with such punk and metal-tinged bands as the Sabians and Shiny Empire) was consistently reflective of his spiritual frameworks. His most explicitly Christian project came about in 2015, when Marler, inspired and horrified by the suffering of persecuted Christians (and other displaced persons) in Syria, recorded an album of traditional hymns with punk rock arrangements as part of a one-off studio project called *The Quick and the Dead*, the proceeds of which continue to support displaced Syrian refugees (some of which Marler and his family have also housed).[26] In recent interviews, however, Marler has increasingly voiced doubts about both his own future in music and, relatedly, the extent to which Orthodox Christians should seek to consume secular music (and even sacred music explicitly appropriating secular genres, such as "Christian punk"). This is one of many data points that make clear that Death to the World does not operate primarily with a logic of appropriation or blending secular/counterculture forms and Christian content, and in this respect the movement is very different from both "contemporary Christian" music (CCM) and its subculture counterparts in "Christian punk" and "Christian metal."[27] The aesthetic ethos of Death to the World is, at least as articulated by Marler and later Valadez, one of gradual replacement of the secular with the sacred, of the subculture with ecclesial culture, and not their melding.[28]

---

26. Cf. Deborah Sengupta Stith, "The Unbroken Circle." As this story makes clear, much of the media attention around Marler foregrounds the "punk to monk" angle still.

27. For excellent studies on attempts at this blending, cf. Marcus Moberg, *Christian Metal: History, Ideology, Scene* (London: Bloomsbury, 2015) and Ibrahim Abraham (ed.), *Christian Punk: Identity and Performance* (London: Bloomsbury, 2020).

28. We can note that, despite Fr. Seraphim Rose's engagement throughout his life with popular culture (including music, television, etc.), this ethic of replacement rather than melding is consistent with his theological understanding of aesthetics as well. A representative passage comes from his widely shared 1982 lecture (just a few years before his death), "Living the Orthodox Worldview:" "But what, one might ask, does all this have to do with us, who are trying to lead, as best we can, a sober Orthodox Christian life? It has a lot to do with it. We have to realize that the life around us, abnormal though it is, is the

Having stepped back in recent years from music, Marler has instead emphasized writing. He is currently engaged in two projects whose connection to the trajectory of Death to the World is clear. First, he is currently completing an updated second edition of *Youth of the Apocalypse*, the context of which is the digital age and new possibilities for sin to take hold in these spaces (a subject that has increasingly been a preoccupation of the zine's writers as well).[29]

Second, he has developed a website (including a T-shirt) centered on a modern updating of the spiritual classic shared between East and West, *Unseen Warfare*, a book originally written by sixteenth-century Venetian Roman Catholic priest Lorenzo Scupoli but later edited by St. Nicodemus of Mt. Athos to bring its content more closely aligned with Orthodoxy. Marler, whose recent intellectual interests have centered on the development of virtues as part of spiritual and civic life, has

---

place where we begin our own Christian life. Whatever we make of our life, whatever truly Christian content we give it, it still has something of the stamp of the 'me generation' on it, and we have to be humble enough to see this. This is where we begin.

There are two false approaches to the life around us that many often make today, thinking that somehow this is what Orthodox Christians should be doing. One approach—the most common one—is simply to go along with the times: adapt yourself to rock music, modern fashions and tastes, and the whole rhythm of our jazzed-up modern life. Often the more old-fashioned parents will have little contact with this life and will live their own life more or less separately, but they will smile to see their children follow after its latest craze and think that this is something harmless.

This path is total disaster for the Christian life; it is the death of the soul. Some can still lead an outwardly respectable life without struggling against the spirit of the times, but inwardly they are dead or dying; and—the saddest thing of all—their children will pay the price in various psychic and spiritual disorders and sicknesses which become more and more common. One of the leading members of the suicide cult that ended so spectacularly in Jonestown four years ago was the young daughter of a Greek Orthodox priest; satanic rock groups like Kiss—'Kids in Satan's Service'—are made up of ax-Russian Orthodox young people; the largest part of the membership of the temple of Satan in San Francisco, according to a recent sociological survey—is made up of Orthodox boys. These are only a few striking cases; most Orthodox young people don't go so far astray—they just blend in with the anti-Christian world around them and cease to be examples of any kind of Christianity for those around them.

This is wrong. The Christian must be different from the world, above all from today's weird, abnormal world, and this must be one of the basic things he knows as part of his Christian upbringing. Otherwise there is no point in calling ourselves Christian—much less Orthodox Christians." Seraphim Rose, "Living the Orthodox Worldview," transcript accessed May 27, 2023, https://classicalchristianity.com/2011/11/19/fr-seraphim-roses-orthodox-world-view/.

29. Cf. especially Marler's comments in "Youth of the Apocalypse with Justin Marler," interview by The Mad Ones.

developed the website with such categories as "The Passions," "The Battlefield," and "Tactics and Methods."

Movingly, the website has featured several writings on virtue written to his young children navigating minefields of growing up that in some ways are reminiscent of his path and are, in other ways, so very different.[30] Proving once again, perhaps, that even more so than concerns with nihilism and apocalypticism, the desire for youth to seek God and be healed is the true through line of his life and ministry.

---

30. Cf. Marler, accessed May 27, 2023, https://www.unseenwarfare.net/.

Chapter 3

REVIVAL AND INFLUENCE

Our society is like that of the Garasenes. When Christ was in their land, He cured a possessed man and cast the demons within him into a herd of swine. The swine then ran off of a cliff and drowned in the sea, causing the herdsman to run with fear into a nearby town. The people of the town, hearing what happened, went out to meet Christ and encountered the once possessed man sane and clothed again before His feet. The people were struck with fear and begged Christ to leave their country. The curing of a madman struck fear in them and it disturbed their way of life. They would've rather lived with the possessed, the mad, or the insane, than to have sanity, purity, and love in their presence. Today, our world reflects this same attitude. With open arms it embraces madness, nurtures it on the breast of apathy, and has raised it as the parent of post-modern culture.

—Father John Valadez[1]

Stirrings of Revival

Anyone who has been to the boardwalk of Venice Beach in Venice, CA, knows that it is a human carnival of epic proportions. In addition to merchandise of the souvenir and chemical variety, all sorts of philosophies, movements, and lifestyles are on display in vendor and human form. It is a true American marketplace in the weirdest possible sense.

Turbo Qualls, a young African American punk rocker and tattoo artist who was a significant presence in various Southern California counterculture scenes, was making his way down the boardwalk when he spotted a booth manned by what appeared to be a wizard: white beard, black cassock, and indifferent air. Intrigued, Qualls went to the booth, where he discovered signs about Eastern Orthodoxy and copies of the zine *Death to the World*.[2]

---

1. Valadez, "Madness," *Death to the World* 25 (2014).

2. The story, as well as other reflections by Fr. Turbo Qualls on his entry into Orthodoxy and its intersections with subculture generally and *Death to the World* specifically, was told to podcaster Buck Johnson on his "Counterflow" podcast. Cf. Buck Johnson, "It Takes

While Qualls was intrigued, it wouldn't be until years later that the memory of his flipping through the zine and being intrigued would come back to him even as he was being drawn, fatefully, into the orbit of the zine and the movement that he would help revive. The significance of the *Death to the World* zine being a presence in his very first encounter with Orthodoxy would not be lost on him.

Years later, Qualls' lifelong interest in counterculture had, in a manner not entirely dissimilar to Marler, taken a more directly spiritual turn. Although raised nominally Protestant, like Marler he was dissatisfied by what he took to be the mainstream respectability of much Protestantism. After various sojourns in the occult and New Age, he eventually founded a highly influential Bible study connected to Goodfella's Tattoo Parlor in Orange, California. The study drew heavily on young people involved in the Christian punk scene centered around Orange County and Los Angeles, and it quickly grew to over fifty people. After the tattoo parlor would close on a Monday night around 10 p.m., the study would begin, and sometimes last until dawn. While the texts and topics under consideration varied, one theme was consistent: the search for an authentic, Acts-based Christianity that would be more authentic than the mainstream, respectable American Christianity on offer.

One of the attendees of the Bible study was John Valadez, who had been drawn both into the punk scene as a disaffected youth and, increasingly, into the Christian punk scene as a spiritual seeker.[3] A regular at shows in which, following a hardcore, thrashing punk set, bands would break out acoustic guitars and lead the assembly in contemporary worship and praise music, Valadez felt himself dissatisfied with his spiritual state. "There was an aspect of Protestant Christianity, at least in my encounter with it, that I didn't feel rejected the world enough," he said. "I didn't feel it rejected fake society enough."[4]

A number of the bands in this scene, such as Headnoise and Officer Negative, were writing lyrics with deeply apocalyptic themes. Once, when one of the bands in the scene was relocating from California to Illinois, it was discovered that they had multiple issues of *Death to the World* amongst their notes. Eventually, Valadez would discover that the zine, which had ceased printing in 1998, was a secret influence upon these evangelical bands who might have been reluctant to disclose the source of their inspiration because it likely would have raised suspicion (as it

---

Humility to Understand What's Happening, with Father Turbo Qualls," *Counterflow*, July 17, 2022, https://deathtotyrants.libsyn.com/ep-217-it-takes-humility-to-understand-whats-happening-with-father-turbo-qualls.

3. As with Marler, details of Valadez's life shared here, unless otherwise noted, are primarily taken from both personal conversations with the author and podcasts: Floridoxy, "John Valadez and Death to the World," and A Devotional Heart, "Father John Valadez on 'Death to the World,' Fr. Seraphim Rose, Fr. Nektarios, and Fr. Turbo," accessed May 27, 2023, https://www.youtube.com/watch?v=v9XeeHIcBjk&t=2013s.

4. Quoted in Emily Brown, "Death to the World: The Last True Rebellion."

did with Valadez at first) that some of the content—particularly focusing on saints, monks, and ascetic practices—was "too Catholic" to pass muster in Protestant circles.

In the meantime, while the bible study at Goodfella's tattoo parlor and the Christian punk shows were spiritually meaningful to Valadez and his friends, they could not function as real ecclesial communities. Monday nights at the study and Friday nights at the clubs might have been sorted out, but Sunday morning remained a void. And the very lack of ecclesial centering characteristic of this sort of experimental Evangelical culture was starting to become part of the problem.

The story of Marina Crissman, who was instrumental along with Valadez in the early days of the zine's renewal, is emblematic:

> I was raised in an evangelical charismatic Christian denomination called Open Bible in Los Angeles, but I began to drift away when I was about sixteen. I believed in God, in Jesus Christ, and in the Bible, but the emotionalism somehow felt wrong. In high school I was very involved in the Christian punk scene. I'd go to the shows, listen to all of the bands and wore shirts that said, "Dead to the World," "No religion, just Christ," and "Religion kills, Jesus saves." This was before I'd even seen the [*Death to the World*] zine, but I was already affected by it. When I finally saw a copy, I understood immediately what I'd picked up on. After high school, I moved to Orange County, where my friend Turbo Qualls led a weekly Bible study for fifty young Christians interested in art and punk music at Turbo's tattoo shop. John was a part of this also. This was part of a stream of alternative, counter-culture churches becoming popular in the evangelical circles.[5]

Meanwhile, Qualls' life and ministry continued to intersect with Orthodoxy, including a fateful encounter at the home of the family of his wife's employer, who were Orthodox. Upon encountering a large icon of Christ in the foyer of the home, Qualls the artist was entranced, and the materials on Orthodoxy that the family gave him to read called to mind the fateful encounter with Orthodoxy—and *Death to the World*—on the Venice Beach boardwalk years earlier. As he dove deeper into study, one of the books he read was *Youth of the Apocalypse*.[6] After a long period of intense discernment, Qualls announced to the Bible study that he was going to become a catechumen in the Orthodox church, and that the (heretofore Protestant) Monday night study would have to cease. However, Qualls' journey and testimony inaugurated a period of spiritual seeking among many of the fifty-plus Bible study attendees, including Valadez (who by that time was also working

---

5. Quoted in Marina Crissman and John Valdez, "Death to the World: An Orthodox Punk Zine Revived and Revisited," interviewed by Geraldine Fagan and RTE.

6. Cf. Fr. John Peck, "Full Impact Faith: An Interview with Fr. Turbo Qualls," accessed May 27, 2023, https://journeytoorthodoxy.com/2017/07/full-impact-faith-an-interview-with-fr-turbo-qualls/.

as an apprentice tattoo artist under Qualls' at the latter's shop). The conditions for revival were set.

Fr. John reflects on the moment in a testimony later printed in the zine:

> I was born into brokenness. I have never known the type of family you read about in books or see in movies. My parents were both very young and separated before I took my first breath of air. They were both metal-heads that had no idea what a baby was all about. Drug use, partying, and cranking up the volume on their stereos was life before me. In fact, my first concert was Iron Maiden while still in the womb and most pictures of my parents before I was born show them clad in Judas Priest and Floyd shirts. Fortunately for me, my parents are indeed very loving and they learned how to sacrifice and take responsibility for the life they brought into the world. From early on, I was used to Black Sabbath screeching from my father's cassette player while we flew down the street in his VW. However, it was not until I was older did Ozzy's words begin to resonate in me as I grappled with the reality of God.
>
> I cannot say when, or where, or how, but beginning in my teenage years I yearned. Can I say I knew what my yearning was for? I am sure some psychologist would assert some assumption as to why, but all I know is that it was genuine. I cannot answer what it was for; I can only pinpoint what it was against. I hated the world. It lacked seriousness and purpose. I began to be incurably annoyed with mundane life and the proposed American dream. As high school years came, influence of new music came. My "crowd" during lunch was behind an unused cafeteria with the punks. It was here that I felt I found a home, a purpose, a rebellion. Through these people I heard Johnny Rotten, Poly Styrene, Beki Bondage, and others that would influence my ways of thinking for years to come. I flew high the banner of "No Future" and the world began to be an even more mundane and dismal place. I related to this rebellion, but I didn't know where it was going. As I attended punk shows, I began to notice the same vanity and mundaneness that we were supposedly rebelling against, except this time it was just masked in Mohawks and studded jackets. Through my high school crowd, I met a guy who was a Christian. He dressed cool, had cool hair, and talked cool, but he was a Christian. He gave me some names of bands and I looked them up, got heavily involved in the Southern California Christian Punk scene and my rebellion became an edgy punkified version of Christianity.
>
> "No compromise! Deny Christ? We'd rather die!" I yelled in the circle pit of an overcrowded Corona venue. I found purpose and an answer to my questions about the unsatisfactory world I saw before me. Show after show got me connected and pulled me into something I felt was radical, real, and worth a true revolution. It became my world and my life. "Jesus Christ Hardcore" was our slogan and we were on a mission for change. Change in the world, change in the churches, and an attempt to change our lives. Then, the scene fell. Band after band moved away, broke up, or left Christ all together. My questions returned, my life had a hole again, and this rebellion, as before, proved to be a shallow one. As Christian punks across SoCal scattered, some found a home, gathering

in a small tattoo shop in Orange and I was one of them. We met on Monday nights when the shop shut down and talked until the early morning about Scripture, the end of the world, society, and change. Lofty talks about Christian communities and revolution filled our heads. We sought to re-find the Church of Acts or rebuild it. This is how Orthodoxy was discovered.

As the tattoo guns were put down and the neon "Open" light was shut off, we gathered for what we didn't know was our last gathering. Some of the group, including our head, had converted and were accepted as Catechumens into Eastern Orthodoxy. As it was announced to us, we were in shock. Because the term was even so foreign to us, many panicked, judged, and the sheep were again scattered. The bible study and parlor gathering would cease and I left that night with a very heavy heart. Back then, Orthodoxy online was not very palatable for seekers, but I did everything I could to wrap my head around what was going on. I had just become the tattoo apprentice to our bible study leader, Turbo, who announced his conversion and needed to know what my friends were into. While doing my research for months, Turbo and I realized that the Christian punk bands that we highly supported had run into Orthodox monks and received *Death to the World* 'zines. We found out where the 'zines were printed and the Abbot of the Monastery sent us a box full of issues. It was in that box was that I first read the line, "The Last True Rebellion." It was simple, I found truth. That was my yearning, truth as a person, Jesus Christ, and the Church built on the blood of unwavering martyrs, Holy Orthodoxy.[7]

In a manner reminiscent of Marler, Valadez went to the relatively paltry sections on Orthodoxy at his local libraries. One of the books that he found was Mathewes-Green's aforementioned text mentioning Death to the World, *At the Corner of East and Now*. Intrigued by her discussion of the original zine and its related coffee shops and bookstores, Valadez and Crissman connected with St. Herman monastery, now under the leadership of Abbot Gerasim (former monastic brother of Marler and spiritual son of Seraphim Rose). While the monastery, after Marler's departure, continued to sell the zine and *Youth of the Apocalypse* at its bookstore, no new issues had been produced for close to a decade. Gerasim gave the young inquirers a box full of zine issues from the 1994–8 run as well as the monastery's seven last copies of *Youth of the Apocalypse*.

By now determined to become catechumens themselves, Valadez and company immediately resumed the spirit of the original movement and began copying and distributing the zines at church punk shows and venues (including, eventually, the massive Christian music festival Cornerstone in Bushnell, IL, where they also featured a prayer booth for daily liturgies amidst the evangelical-oriented festival). Again, with zines, this distribution is easily done by design: a quick staple removal and trip to Kinkos, and distribution could be easily achieved.

---

7. John Valadez, "Arriving at the Last True Rebellion," accessed August 14, 2022, https://deathtotheworld.com/articles/arriving-at-the-last-true-rebellion/.

Meanwhile, a fertile conversation was beginning with the erstwhile punk Protestant group—over the next several years, dozens became catechumens. The main parish location for their reception was St. Barnabas (Antiochian) in Costa Mesa, CA, which quickly became known as a "spiritual hospital" (a common Orthodox designation for the church, following St. John Chrysostom's oft-quoted maxim that the church is "not a courtroom for sinners but a hospital for the ill") in which a host of tattooed, pierced inquirers would gather to experience the liturgy and learn about the faith. St. Barnabas would soon fain another reputation—as a parish producing a number of seminarians and eventually priests. Within a few years, Qualls and Valadez were on their way to ordinations, first as deacons and then as priests.

However, the crew busily distributing *Death to the World* zines at shows were eager for fresh content; unfortunately, the monks at St. Herman by this point were not in a position to produce new *Death to the World* issues (being busy with the ongoing production of *The Orthodox Word* and other publishing ventures, and perhaps bereft of monks with quite the same instincts for counterculture-friendly content as Marler). In response, however, Abbott Gerasim decided to bless an experiment. He invited Valadez, Crissman, and other interested writers and artists to draft a new issue of *Death to the World* (what would become Issue #13) and send it to the monastery for approval. They did, and after some editorial changes the monks blessed the issue and approved it for distribution in 2006.

The New Context

We might ask, at this point, what difference the changed context between the late 1990s and the twenty-first century might have meant for the project of reviving *Death to the World*. While in the long-term scheme of things, the intervening years between the late 1990s and the early 2000s may not seem like a long enough time for significant shifts to have occurred, in an era of what sociologist Hartmut Rosa has termed the "age of acceleration" (technologically and socially), and in the rapidly changing context(s) of US religion in the internet age, the relative brevity of any given span of time may nonetheless contain a host of massive changes.[8]

In his 1994 text *Authority: Construction and Corrosion*, eminent historian of religion Bruce Lincoln describes (somewhat presciently for a book written long before anyone might have fully grasped what the internet would become) of the fragmentation of authority into diffuse "stages"[9]—what we might today call "platforming." As has already been mentioned and will be discussed further below,

---

8. Cf. Hartmut Rosa, *Social Acceleration: A New Theory of Modernity*, trans. Jonathan Trejo-Mathys (New York: Columbia Press, 2015).

9. Bruce Lincoln, *Authority: Construction and Corrosion* (Chicago: University of Chicago Press, 1995).

Eastern Orthodoxy in the United States and globally represents a particularly intense case of this diffusion—with no magisterium and with ecclesiology largely inextricable from the vagaries of national context. However, also salient in an internet age is not simply diffusion, but what we might call algorithmic clustering.

To understand how algorithmic clustering impacts religion and culture, we might imagine a thought experiment that asks the following question: what do insistence upon the inerrancy and infallibility of the Bible, support for the rights of American citizens to own assault rifles, opposition to legalized abortion, support for the death penalty, tolerance/promotion of the US flag being displayed in church sanctuaries and the Ten Commandments being displayed in public schools, and opposition to amnesty for undocumented immigrants have in common? At a purely conceptual level, the answer would have to be, "nothing." There are no necessary connections (and indeed, on first blush, some noticeable tensions) among these positions. That said, most who pay attention to the news in the United States would recognize that this bundle of stances characterizes a high percentage of white Evangelical Christian conservatives in this country (and, consequently, a sizable portion of the Republican party's base demographic).[10] This is due at least in part to the fact that, when it comes to how views on religion and "culture war" issues intersect, few if any of us operate from positions of strict logical necessity or syllogistic coherence; rather, as both historians and such "genealogical" thinkers as Michel Foucault have shown us, there are contingent but very real historical variables and interests that go into how we bundle our beliefs (and also how, within these bundles, the various views end up reinforcing and amplifying each other).

This has significant implications for how theology interacts with other discourses. Sociologist Robert Wuthnow pointed out decades ago that, in US Christianity, culture war positioning long ago outpaced theology or denominational allegiance as the key factor in Christian association.[11] While this should not necessitate absolute cynicism when it comes to the importance of theology, it does remind us of its limits. Moreover, in an age of social media and increased arbitration of matters theological and cultural online, historically contingent interests and factors are accelerated immeasurably by the technological design factors that make up the modern internet.[12] The algorithms that drive social media and make the platforms profitable and authoritative (ala Lincoln)—with their deployment of advertisements and "click" analytics—incentivize the "rabbit trails" of sustained attention. The algorithmic chain makes the profit by doing the bundling, and this far more than logic (or theo-logic) drives much of the chain of associations.

---

10. Cf. Andrew L. Whitehead and Samuel L. Perry, *Taking America Back for God: Christian Nationalism in the United States* (Oxford: Oxford University Press, 2022).

11. Cf. Robert Wuthnow, *The Restructuring of American Religion: Society and Faith since World War II* (Princeton, NJ: Princeton University Press, 1988).

12. Cf. Justin E. H. Smith, *The Internet Is Not What You Think It Is: A History, A Philosophy, A Warning* (Princeton, NJ: Princeton University Press, 2022).

Why does this matter in the case of *Death to the World*'s re-emergence as a theological publication in a suddenly online world? Algorithmic bundling accelerates the blurring of religious and political lines. When the zine began, the novel but resonant affinities between punk rock/metal cultures and Rose-style Orthodoxy was justification enough to try the experiment; however, the technological realities on the ground in 2006 became the stage for what has in fact happened: the incorporation of *Death to the World*'s theo-aesthetic into algorithmically amplified/accelerated clusters that draw on the affective energy of punk rock and the apocalyptic fervor of Rose-style Orthodoxy in order to link Orthodoxy with impulses that are, in some cases, reactionary both politically and theologically. In other words, *Death to the World*'s reboot happened at a time in which its core themes of rebellion and apocalypse could find themselves recruited to—and thus lending aesthetic and theological weight toward—the similarly apocalyptic and even conspiratorial themes that animate much US Orthodoxy (particularly in its online forms) today. The stage was set for the mixture of theology and politics to become even more intensely charged. We will have more to say about this in the next chapter.

Expansion

The experiment of the early issues would prove a success, and the need for sign-off from St. Herman would soon cease. Valadez and his fellow creatives brought an entrepreneurial energy to the zine utilizing technologies that were nascent at the close of the previous run but were crucial for content production in the new millennium. The 1990s had word of mouth; the twenty-first century had website traffic.

In addition to regularizing publication of new zine issues (up to #28 as of this writing), two moves were particularly significant. First, shortly after conceiving the first issue in 2006, the new team put together a website for both issue-based writings and, eventually, web-exclusive articles. As Duncombe has noted, the DIY reproducibility and outsider ethos of zine culture were, in many respects, a precursor to the web, which (ostensibly) is a free-range marketplace of equal access to ideas wherein even the most niche content, under the right circumstances, might go "viral."[13] To be sure, it is unlikely that this is actually how the internet functions. Even absent such a fully idealized conception of net neutrality, though, there is no question that the online reach of *Death to the World*'s website took its reach to levels unfathomable by even the most diligent physical zine distributors.

Second, as indicated in the introduction to this book, Valadez and his collaborators dramatically expanded the range of merchandise branded with Death to the World logos and images, which also meant commissioning new art

---

13. Duncombe, *Notes from Underground*, esp. the "Afterword" to the second edition.

regularly. The original *Death to the World* run featured a grand total of one T-shirt (the aforementioned cover image of Elder Nikodemus holding a skull from Issue #1); since 2006, by contrast, over thirty distinct shirt designs (plus hoodies, pins, stickers, bags, flags, and so on—all fixtures of material punk culture) have been produced and sold via the website.

We referred above to Thompson's notion of the varied modes of punk textuality coalescing into a "punk project;" here we can augment this by utilizing music theorist David Toop's term "sonic cultures" that surround the choice (conscious or not) to equate consuming certain forms of music with identity formation, along with other attendant signifiers of consumption and representation (e.g., fashion, events, social networks).[14] When music is life, then music is never just about music; it is about life and identity in all its aspects. If the original Death to the World idea hinged on the proposition that youth emerging from punk and metal subcultures would recognize and resonate with the dark aesthetic presentation of Orthodox content offered by the zine, then the current "second wave" of Death to the World amplifies that impulse by extending it to other realms of "punk textuality." The result is a level of social cohesion and recognizability across otherwise disparate sectors (by class, race, ecclesial location, and so on) by means of shared appreciation, consumption, and visible display of objects participating in a discernible subcultural logic.[15] Punk style is not just "rebellion;" it is also—especially in cases like Death to the World—a material vehicle for shared resonance and cultural collaboration. But it is one haunted by instabilities: is the rebellion perpetual? Can the tools of mainstream culture be employed with any authenticity toward the task of encapsulating and disseminating (perhaps even "selling") the rebellion?

Melding or Replacement?

As indicated earlier with Marler, moreover, there is another kind of tension in this strategy. This is because Valadez in particular has expressed agreement with Marler that the goal of Death to the World is not to bring Orthodoxy into punk/metal subcultures in order to inflect the music or the scene with, say, Orthodox lyrical content, or to produce some kind of melding of the ecclesial and secular cultures. Instead, the goal is to gradually draw subculture adherents out of what Valadez sees as "empty" modes of rebelling that characterize these scenes. The website of the parish where Valadez serves as priest even gives the following one-sentence description in its link to the Death to the World website: "A zine and online presence for teens and young adults who are entrapped in music scenes

---

14. Cf. Toop, *Ocean of Sound*.

15. Cf. Dick Hebdige's seminal 1979 text *Subculture: The Meaning of Style* (London: Routledge, 1988) as well as David Muggleton, *Inside Subculture: The Postmodern Meaning of Style* (Oxford: Berg, 2002).

and subculture and are looking for truth in a dark world in uncertain times."[16] If this is true, however, then how does this square, not only with Death to the World itself engaging in material productions recognizable within these subcultures (because patterned after them)—not to mention inspiring a host of other merchants and artists (discussed below) to do the same?

Here again we can note that this tension is a particularly spiritual variation on a longstanding and broad debate within punk culture in particular: if the punk ethos is ultimately concerned with the rebellion of unvarnished truth (be it theological as in the case of Death to the World, or secular) against phoniness and hypocrisy, and if so much of that phoniness is tied in with the consumerist edifice of modern American life (which many scholars and punk activists would identify as the outworking of neoliberal late capitalist impulses[17]), then can the house of lies really be brought down (to paraphrase Audre Lorde) with its own tools? Can "hip" or "punk" consumption be a spiritual antidote to the emptiness of consumer society? Can rebellion be purchased? Placing Death to the World's particular theological tensions within this broader history of contestation does not solve the aporia, but it does show how these tensions are endemic to the sort of enterprise that the movement has pursued. We will consider these questions more directly in this book's conclusion.

In the case of Death to the World, we can notice that this replacement ethic (as articulated by Marler and Valadez) is not necessarily shared either by all of its fans or even by all of the creatives inspired by it; for instance, in his art and public comments Christian Grimm of 13th Vigil (discussed below) has demonstrated more comfort with conceiving of his work as demonstrating how Orthodoxy can live alongside (in his case) black metal fandom.[18] It is perhaps more analytically accurate, then, to say that, even if the original impulses of Death to the World's chief instigators and re-instigators were to advance a replacement agenda, as the movement has expanded and diversified this ethic lives alongside other negotiations between participation in Orthodox culture and counterculture. Fr. Turbo Qualls has spoken about the ways in which his formation in countercultures of various kinds (metal, punk, anime, even occult) prepared him for occupying Orthodoxy itself as counterculture,[19] and it is safe to say that the outworking of these dual formations continues to vary among Death to the World fans.

---

16. John Valadez, "Other Resources," *St. Timothy Orthodox Church*, May 4, 2019, http://www.sttimothy.net/index.php/2019/05/04/other-resources/.

17. Cf. Mark Fisher, *Capitalist Realism: Is There No Alternative?* (London: Zero Books, 2009).

18. Cf. Robert Saler and Kevin Clay, "Christian Grimm of 13th Vigil on Art of the Apocalypse," accessed May 27, 2023, https://www.youtube.com/watch?v=b_Fq1g2wWT8&t=8s.

19. Johnson, "It Takes Humility to Understand What's Happening."

It is important to note, too, in connection with the question of economics: both with music and in media, selling physical merchandise in order to keep content relatively free and accessible (and thus not vulnerable to the whims of the intellectual marketplace itself, as for instance in the case of online "clickbait" news) has a long and venerable history. As Tim Wu has pointed out, if consumers are not willing to consciously support content production financially, then that content will inevitably be shaped to capture their attention—with attention itself the commodity that is traded.[20] In more recent years, this reality has led to the rise of more fan-supported business models such as Substack and Patreon (the latter of which Death to the World has recently joined), and it may be that in movements like Death to the World the growing sophistication and popularity of these models may lead to less dependence on merchandise to support the zine content (which of course would not in and of itself settle the question as to whether the same level of merch production "ought" to happen). In its current iteration—unlike with the first run, which had the benefit of monastery infrastructure to support its production—Death to the World is, economically speaking, the sole property of Valadez (the monks having ceded rights to profits early on in the revival); thus, it is likely that the zines continued existence will remain dependent on creative funding models beyond distribution of the zine content itself.

Bearing Rose's Legacy

The consolidation of Death to the World's operations within Valadez's editorial and financial oversight has been accompanied by increasing links between the website (including its social media presence on Facebook and Instagram in particular) and Valadez's educational ministry, including at the parish where he has served as priest for several years (St. Timothy Antiochian Orthodox Church in Lompoc, CA). And in an internet age, the prospect of a parish in California serving as a spiritual home base for a worldwide movement is fully plausible. Many Orthodox priests offer teaching and even lecture content at their parishes, and within the US context such outlets as Ancient Faith Radio have been at the forefront of turning some of this content into podcasts. True to the DIY spirit, however, the social media savvy Valadez has focused on developing his own channels for disseminating lectures whose theology and subject matter are highly consonant with Death to the World.

In particular, he has offered updated, contemporized versions of Rose's aforementioned "Orthodox Survival Course" and lectures on "The Soul after Death" (the Rose versions of which contain the statements for which Rose is perhaps best known within Orthodox circles, in which he endorses and considerably expounds

---

20. Cf. Timothy Wu, *The Attention Merchants: The Epic Scramble to Get inside Our Heads* (New York: Knopf, 2016). We might think too of the number of churches, especially in Western Europe, that depend financially on the sale of religious souvenirs and other material goods for their financial viability as institutions.

upon the existence of "aerial toll houses," or demonic obstacles that the soul must face after death en route to judgment).[21] Valadez's updates of Rose in these contexts could in fact double as a restatement of Death to the World's commitment to discerning "the signs of the times":

> Today we are Orthodox. Our Orthodoxy is like a little island amidst a great sea of different ideologies and different lifestyles and different ways just of how to think and interact with the world. And more and more our island is becoming smaller and smaller in this great vast ocean that is the world. So unfortunately, values of this world have been going astray from an Orthodox holistic outlook and you know life. So it's important that we have to be, you know, we have to be engaging with these things, and we have to be aware of these things, and we have to be aware of where the world is going and where it is headed and the ways in which it wants to drag us along with it. So, we have to have an awareness and to deal with matters of our age in an Orthodox manner in order to survive today and not be crippled in some kind of abnormal way or live some kind of abnormal life. We have to develop an outlook on the world that is permeated with the same outlook as the Church Fathers. We have to be aware of the demands also that the world makes upon our souls, and we have to be realistic about them and engage with them and answer them in an Orthodox manner.[22]

As will be discussed in the next chapter, in the last several years this bringing to bear of a critical Orthodox analysis of contemporary events has focused on such controversial topics as Covid-19 compliance and perceived communism in US culture. That said, as noted above in our discussion of Rose, even as the particular topics change with the times, the overall framework on display in Valadez's teaching, whereby Orthodox faithful must be vigilant in watching for apocalyptic signs of nihilism's triumph as a preparation for the antichrist's advent remains very much in Rose's lineage. Thus, in different but complementary ways, both *Death to the World*'s initial and current runs represent a significant preservation and extension of Rose's legacy within US Orthodoxy in particular. And indeed, this ongoing work also keeps alive a spirit of rebellion present in Rose himself:

> Let not us, who would be Christians, expect anything else from it than to be crucified. For to be Christian is to be crucified, in this time and in any time since Christ came for the first time. His life is the example—and warning—to us all. We must be crucified personally, mystically; for through crucifixion is the only

---

21. Many of these lectures can be found at the parish website: John Valadez, "Catechetical School," *St. Timothy Orthodox Church*, accessed May 27, 2023, http://www.sttimothy.net/index.php/category/recordings/.

22. John Valadez, "The Orthodox World View: Spiritual Formation and Discernment Today," *St. Thomas Orthodox Church*, August 13, 2020, http://www.sttimothy.net/index.php/2020/08/13/survival-course-for-orthodox-christians/.

path to resurrection. If we would rise with Christ, we must first be humbled with Him—even to the ultimate humiliation, being devoured and spit forth by the uncomprehending world. And we must be crucified outwardly, in the eyes of the world; for Christ's Kingdom is not of this world, and the world cannot bear it, even a single representative of it, even for a single moment. The world can only accept Antichrist, now or at any time. No wonder, then, that it is hard to be a Christian—it is not hard, it is impossible. No one can knowingly accept a way of life which, the more truly it is lived, leads the more surely to one's own destruction. And that is why we constantly rebel, try to make life easier, try to be half Christian, try to make the best of both words. We must ultimately choose—our felicity lies in one world or the other, not in both. God give us the strength to pursue the path to crucifixion; there is no other way to be a Christian.[23]

Even more recently Valadez has extended the Death to the World brand to new ventures: a podcast named Ek Nekron (taken from the Orthodox Pascha acclamation, "Christ is risen from the dead," or *Christos Anesti Ek Nekron*) which features a mix of the aforementioned St. Timothy lectures as well as Death to the World-specific content, a new Patreon (crowd-funded) page wherein patrons financially supporting Death to the World at various levels can access exclusive content, and *Death to the World En Español*, a Spanish-language translation of selected zine and web articles. While Death to the World has always had popularity in Russia and other traditionally Orthodox countries, this last effort stands as an acknowledgment of the fact that interest in Orthodoxy continues to expand within historically underrepresented populations (including within the United States).

The zine's author base also continues to expand, as more and more priests and laity continue to catch the vision. The enthusiasm is well captured by frequent contributor Owen Schumacher:

For many reasons, it's a unique honor to write for *Death to the World*, a publication whose aim is to touch readers thought unlikely to set foot in a church. In part, I take joy in editing and writing for *Death to the World* because of my own background and journey: As a young man, I was a Protestant with a taste for history and a curiosity to know more; simultaneously, I was an idealistic art student with a love for very loud music. I've never thought of my yearning for Christ and my love for art and music to be antagonistic forces. *Death to the World* is a publication for those who enjoy beauty: in its readers, in its readers' aesthetics, and most importantly, in its God and His saints. It's *Death to the World*'s focused and ardent love for God and His saints that enlivens it; otherwise, *Death to the World* would be some cynical evangelistic tract … Editing for *Death to the World* deepens my participation in the Church, reorients my love of culture, and draws me closer to Christ and His living saints.[24]

---

23. Quoted in Damascene, *Father Seraphim Rose*, 190.
24. Private communication with author, August 2, 2022.

Inspirations

If Death to the World is the acknowledged trailblazer when it comes to the interaction between Orthodoxy and punk culture, and if in the 1990s a number of related enterprises and ministries (such as coffee shops and bookstores) emerged, then the same has occurred in connection with the zine's current revival. Unsurprisingly, to the extent that the current renewal has featured a significant increase in themed clothing and merchandise, many of the new ventures have followed suit. Death to the World is a major inspiration upon online Orthodoxy in the United States.

In the introduction to this book, I named a number of features that I am positing as constitutive of the "Death to the World theo-aesthetic" (including spare color palettes, rebellion against emptiness and falsehood in culture, apocalyptic invocations of spiritual struggle, war against the Antichrist and perceived agents of cultural nihilism, to name just a few). In the following discussion of movements that I am identifying as cognate to Death to the World, it is important to keep this list in mind since not every artist or vendor that I will be discussing is directly engaging musical subcultures (although some do). All of them, however, are operating in the theo-aesthetic trajectory inaugurated by Death to the World.

To start with clothing, Death to the World's influence is discernible upon Orthodoxy Unlimited, a clothing line that features a variety of longstanding (if somewhat martial) Orthodox slogans such as "give me Orthodoxy or give me death" (variations of which, as I will discuss in the conclusion, are common in monasteries) as well as symbols such as the Byzantine eagle—which has associations both with Orthodoxy proper but also Greek nationalism. The line has at various times also featured a variety of contemporary holy figures, including some favored by Death to the World (although, following general Death to the World policy, it does not reproduce actual icons on clothing out of respect for the icon's function in Orthodox piety). Orthodoxy Unlimited's shirt line also has tees with acerbic interventions into contemporary ecclesial debates, such as "ecumenism is heresy" as well as, humorously or bemusingly depending upon your view of academic theology, "Begone Fordhamite," a reference to the Orthodox Christian Studies Center at Fordham University, the United States' most prominent academic site for the study of Orthodoxy but much maligned among conservative Orthodox for their perceived advocacy for "progressive" causes.

More directly, the artist Christian Grimm, creative and proprietor behind the clothing line 13th Vigil (begun in 2021), readily acknowledges the key role played by Death to the World both in his eventual embrace of Orthodoxy from a Protestant background (as well as lifelong participation in both motorcycle and black metal cultures).[25] The owner of Redemption Barber Shop in Dallas, TX, where those getting their hair cut might find themselves draped in a large Seraphim Rose cape

---

25. Cf. The Orthodox Logos, "Interview with Christian Grimm of 13th Vigil," accessed May 28, 2023, https://www.youtube.com/watch?v=4X-urb9PSh0.

to catch falling hair, Grimm was inspired to apply the artistic talents that he had already put to use designing several shirts for Death to the World to his own line, one that would draw more directly on the dark but vibrant colors and spiritual warfare-inspired designs characteristic of heavy metal album covers. To a greater degree than punk or even the relatively minimalist metal characteristic of Marler-era Sleep, metal has long drawn on mythologized and fantasy-laden aesthetics, and 13th Vigil applies this vibe to great effect in what amounts to both a homage to and a furthering of the horizons established by Death to the World. While, as we have seen, "metal" and "punk" tend to be conflated often in discourse around Death to the World and its fans, 13th Vigil embodies a sort of rebellious spirit characteristic of punk imbued with the otherworldliness of metal and, on this construal, of Orthodoxy.

13th Vigil's theological frame also bears traces of Death to the World's influence; in addition to featuring Rose and a number of saints highlighted by the zine (13th Vigil to this point has been less reticent about picturing canonized saints on its designs[26]), a number of shirts have sharp slogans reminiscent of Rose and progeny's agonistic discernment of the "signs of the times," such as "Anti Anti Christ Gun Club" and "Resist the New World Order." Like its predecessor, 13th Vigil represents a material embodiment of the confluence of apocalyptic theology, subculture aesthetic, and ancient Christian hagiography whose plausibility owes much to Death to the World's pioneering.

The most direct renewal of the 1990s coffee shops/bookstores, albeit in primarily web-based form, is California's Punks and Monks Books (begun in 2021), whose logo directly cites the tagline "The Last True Rebellion" and whose site is redolent with Rose quotes, especially his oft-cited admonition, "It is later than you think, hasten therefore to do the work of God!"[27] The books, jewelry, and clothing offered by the store are largely standard fare for Orthodox bookstores (prayer books, saints' writings, modest clothing for women, crosses, etc.), but also feature some more directly Death to the World-recalling shirts such as skulls emblazoned with Eastern crosses and the injunction (in stark red letting on a black shirt) to "Prepare for Death" and a blood-red rendering of Tertullian's maxim (also oft-cited by Death to the World) that "the blood of the martyrs is the seed of the church."

What is most striking about the store, though, is the fact that it has organized into a 501c3 nonprofit outreach organization that has established increasingly close ties to St. Herman's monastery as well as a network of Orthodox jurisdictions abroad. It is fast becoming an online community and not just a store. In this capacity, an increasing part of its mission and business model centers on organizing pilgrimages (to traditional Orthodox countries such as Georgia as well as Platina domestically). Recently, with Valadez's support, the owners have taken on a key role in the American effort to see Rose officially canonized as a saint (discussed below in Chapter 5).

---

26. St. John of Kronstadt, St. Olga, St. Elizabeth the New Martyr, St. Seraphim of Sarov, and St. Joseph the Hesychast are examples. Cf. www.13thvigil.com.

27. https://shop.punksandmonks.com/.

In addition to these more formal enterprises, a major part of the story of Death to the World's growing influence in the twenty-first century and in the US Orthodox scene in particular has been the increasing evidence of the zine's aesthetic impact upon Orthodox online presence, either in the form of direct reference to the "death to the world" ethos (as in the deployment of the hashtag #deathtotheworld attached generally to a spiritual point on the contrast between Orthodoxy and modern life) or in the use by dedicated social media accounts of the aesthetic signifiers that we have been discussing.[28] There are no signs of the use of the phrase slowing down, and those who use it seem to have a fairly unified sense of what they mean when they do. Now, in this case, arguing that there is a direct tie to Death to the World can be difficult; not every "dark" depiction of Orthodox content is necessarily indebted to the zine or movement, since (again) this content and to a certain extent the aesthetic has always been present in the tradition. That said, it is plausible to assert that Death to the World's influence has increased the plausibility and attraction of these theo-aesthetic endeavors, whether there is a direct lineage between the movement and these creators or a more ambient one. As we will discuss in the next chapter, in some cases the social media gestures that draw on Death to the World are tied to particularly contested and fraught Orthodox interventions into contemporary issues of politics and authority, and that fact bears investigating.

That said, on the whole it seems to be the case that, after almost thirty years of Death to the World's project, there seems to be widespread acceptance of the notion that at least a certain subset of contemporary Orthodox believers and seekers continue to benefit spiritually from having the ancient resources of the church presented in somber, counterculture-friendly ways. As we have seen throughout this chapter, this comfort continues to raise core questions of co-existence of ecclesial and subculture versus replacement of one with the other; however, somewhere in the midst of these (perhaps productive) tensions, many are finding resources for their ongoing spiritual struggle and encouragement. Again, Crissman puts it well in describing her decision to participate in the zine's revival:

> [*Death to the World*] was written by young converts who remembered the anguish of not being there. To read what people had gone through before coming to the Church made you feel that you were part of a united front. Not that we necessarily knew each other, but we didn't need to because you felt that they were out there struggling along with you. The lives of saints and martyrs made us aware that no matter what we've gone through, the saints struggled harder. This shone a light on the physical reality of Orthodoxy—it's more than a belief or a feeling, it's a physical part of life.[29]

---

28. At the time of this writing, examples include the (public) accounts of Orthodox Ethos and Orthodox Nepsis.

29. Quoted in "Death to the World: An Orthodox Punk Zine Revived and Revisited."

Chapter 4

WHOSE AUTHORITY TO FIGHT?

In the previous chapters, I have told the story of Death to the World's origins and revival with plenty of theological annotation along the way. In this chapter, I wish to turn more intentionally to some core debates within contemporary Eastern Orthodox Christianity in the United States in order to show how we might see Death to the World both influenced by, and in some cases influential within, them. In particular, I want to think through questions of authority and how it interacts both with the creation of artistic and theological content (as in the case of Death to the World), but also with how a movement like Death to the World intervenes in contestations over authority. If rebellion against authority is the lifeblood of punk, then critique of bad authority and identification of the right sources for obedience has been a core part of the Death to the World story.

Death to the World is a particularly relevant case study since, in the last several years, the zine has taken a more visibly active role in refracting Orthodox views on public tensions under the rubric, ala Rose, of discerning the "signs of the times." Put more directly, since US politics since 2020 have been consumed with controversies over Covid-19 policies, critical race theory (including allegations of Marxism), and other hot-button topics, Death to the World has increasingly brought these topics into its orbit both with zine articles and with art.

Specifically, Death to the World demonstrates a particular Orthodox concern with Marxism (evoking living memories of Soviet persecution of Christians in the twentieth century), with concomitant praise of monarchy (tsarism) as a God-ordained "strongman" restraining communism; moreover, this similar frame has been utilized to raise critical questions about state enforcement of Covid-19 policy, particularly the closing of churches (perhaps most aggressively in California, which is where Death to the World's base of operations resides).

Authority in US Orthodoxy

Even though Death to the World has a global reach, both in its origin and centering it is a US Orthodoxy phenomenon. But what is authority in US Orthodoxy? While it is a huge topic, a few comments are warranted here.

Scholars have approached questions of authority in US Christianity from a number of angles. Some, operating within framework of "religious marketplace" established in the twentieth century by sociologists such as Wade Clark Roof, have focused on conversion as a mode of operationalizing the choice for certain configurations of religious authority.[1] Others have focused on longstanding theological-hermeneutical questions of the tension between textual interpretation (e.g., of scripture) and recognized magisterial authority as embodied in ecclesial hierarchy.[2] Still others have zeroed in on how such "external" factors as white supremacy, anxieties over neoliberal capitalism, and "digital religion" both legitimate and destabilize authoritative religious structures.[3]

Indeed, several of the most prominent recent monographs on US Eastern Orthodoxy have incorporated these themes of conversion, textuality, and juridical authority within their analytic frames.[4] However, this is where the aforementioned noncanonical status of Orthodoxy complicates the application of these frames, and layers on additional complexities related to transnational, geopolitical, and historical realities.

While Eastern Orthodox churches represent themselves as fully unified in terms of both polity (centered around Eucharistic fellowship, which is shared only within canonically recognized Orthodox bodies[5]) and theology (stemming from their adherence to the creedal orthodoxy determined by the seven ecumenical

---

1. Cf. *inter alia* Lincoln A. Mullen, *The Chance of Salvation: A History of Conversion in America* (Cambridge, MA: Harvard, 2017) and Hans Joas, *Faith as an Option: Possible Futures for Christianity* (Palo Alto, CA: Stanford, 2014).

2. Cf. Robert Saler, *Between Magisterium and Marketplace* (Minneapolis, MN: Fortress Press, 2014).

3. Cf. Anthea Butler, *White Evangelical Racism: The Politics of Morality in America* (Chapel Hill, NC: UNC Press, 2021); R. Marie Griffith, *Moral Combat: How Sex Divided American Christians and Fractured American Politics* (New York: Basic, 2017); Heidi A. Campbell, *Digital Creatives and the Rethinking of Religious Authority* (New York: Routledge, 2020).

4. Three significant monographs in this regard are Amy Slagle, *The Eastern Orthodox Church in the Spiritual Marketplace: American Conversions to Orthodox Christianity* (DeKalb, IL: Northern Illinois University Press, 2011); Herbel, *Turning to Tradition*; Sarah Riccardi-Swartz, *Between Heaven and Russia: Religious Conversion and Political Apostasy in Appalachia* (New York: Fordham, 2022).

5. Hence the aforementioned difficulties with determining the extent to which "Oriental" Orthodox (which encompass such large global churches as those in Egypt (Coptic) and most of Africa) should be counted as Orthodox for analytic purposes, since canonical Eastern churches (which recognize the authority of the Council of Chalcedon's teaching on monophysitism) and "Oriental" Orthodox churches (which do not) are not in Eucharistic communion with each other, even though they share a good deal of institutional cooperation (e.g., Oriental Orthodox seminarians in the United States are trained at the (Eastern) Orthodox Church in America's flagship seminary, St. Vladimir's in New York).

councils, held between the years 325–787), there is no equivalent to a magisterium or pope in Orthodoxy (while the Patriarch of Constantinople is given the honorific "Ecumenical Patriarch," his actual jurisdiction is geographically small and relatively resource-poor compared to that of the largest Patriarchate, Moscow). Instead, the canonical vision of Orthodoxy is that each geographic territory (roughly but not exactly corresponding to recognized nationhood) has its own independent (or autocephalous) church, with the bishop/metropolitan/patriarch (the title varies depending, among other things, on the size and historical prestige of the church) having full authority over the liturgical, spiritual, and canonical life of the church in the territory. In other words, Orthodox unity is, ideally, comprised by the unity of independent churches in distinct geographic territories—many independent churches operating Eucharistically as one across the globe. Hence, canonically, there should be one church in Greece, one in Romania, one in Russia, and so on.

As one can imagine, though, multiple factors complicate the actual outworking of this ideal both historically and in the present. For one, as mentioned above, the recognition of autocephaly within a given church by the other autocephalous church is tricky when the independent status of the nation is in question, or when there are questions as to whether the territory is significant enough to maintain its own national church (or when, as in the case of recent controversies in the Ukraine, a neighboring church—Moscow—has a great deal of wealth and membership to lose if the Ukrainian church is granted autocephaly and thus institutional independence from the Moscow Patriarchate).[6] Thus, significant divisions and even minor schisms have arisen in the church when, for instance, the Estonian Orthodox church has been recognized as autocephalous by the Ecumenical Patriarch but not Moscow, or when the Orthodox Church in America (a relatively small offshoot of the Russian Church) has been recognized as autocephalous by Moscow but not Constantinople, or—consequentially—when the Ecumenical Patriarch grants a *tomos* (certificate of autocephaly) to the Ukrainian Orthodox Church against the stated wishes of the Moscow Patriarchate, as happened in 2019 as a significant precursor to present conflict between Russia and the Ukraine.

These geopolitical tensions shed some light on why, in a comparatively young immigrant nation such as the United States, the "mother" or ethnic churches that sponsored missions to the United States (such as the Russian missions to Alaska in the late eighteenth and early nineteenth centuries) and kept ties with ethnic immigrant enclaves in the United States such as the Greeks, Lebanese, Romanians, Slavs, etc. have never been able to agree upon the constitution of a single unified US Orthodox Church. Canonically, the present situation in which a drive around Indianapolis and its north suburbs might find the car passing a Greek Orthodox Church (Holy Trinity in Carmel), an Antiochian Orthodox Church (St. George in Fishers), a Romanian church (Sts. Constantine and Helena on the near north side) should not exist—all of these should be parishes within the same US jurisdiction.

---

6. Cf. Nicholas Denysenko, *The Orthodox Church in Ukraine: A Century of Separation* (Ithaca, NY: Cornell University Press, 2018).

The aforementioned Orthodox Church in America represents one attempt (stemming from the 1970s) to organize such a church, but as mentioned above its autocephaly has been recognized by some Patriarchates (e.g., Moscow) but not others, with the latter including the Ecumenical Patriarchate.

The absence of magisterial authority characteristic of Protestantism, existing in tension with representations of ecclesial unity reminiscent of Roman Catholicism, layered in with built-in geopolitical considerations rather unique (at least in their intensity) within Eastern Orthodoxy, makes for a complex and consequential series of instabilities when it comes to US Orthodoxy. Two examples can illustrate this phenomenon.

One, in the late 1980s, a group of evangelicals connected to Campus Crusade for Christ undertook a study of the early church and decided, after much debate, that they needed to incorporate Orthodox liturgy, icons, clergy structures, and other Eastern signifiers into their still-Protestant church movement. These parishes, known collectively as the Evangelical Orthodox Church in America (EOC), undertook a spiritual odyssey that eventually led most of them to seek admittance *en masse* into the canonical Eastern Orthodox church.[7] In an institutional enactment of the complexities of the spiritual marketplace, the EOC parishes first petitioned the Greeks (who were apparently suspicious of their motives), then found a home for some of their parishes in the Antiochian church, then saw a second wave of churches join the OCA, all while some parishes remained in the EOC and still represent themselves to (no doubt bewildered) outsiders as "Orthodox" even as they maintain fully Protestant self-determination.

Second, and perhaps more consequentially, lack of centeredness can lead to slow responses to threats. When Matthew Heimbach (a white supremacist connected to a parish in Bloomington, IN, before being excommunicated for, among other things, his key role in organizing the 2017 "Unite the Right" rally in Charlottesville, VA) lost his official status as an Orthodox Christian in good Eucharistic standing, a major problem was revealed: the relative chaos and de-centeredness of US Orthodoxy meant (and means) that it has been very difficult for Orthodox parishes existing in close geographic proximity but in separate jurisdictions to track the movement of white supremacist/alt-right Orthodox from parish to parish. Indeed, Heimbach and his followers' case demonstrates a further layer of complexity to this diffusion: the fact that within US Orthodoxy, like in so many other US expressions of Christianity, much of the de facto authority, community, and formation have moved online, where it is even less subject to directly church oversight. Lack of centralized authority can mean that things—and bad actors—can slip through the cracks.

The point to all this is that, when it comes to authority in US Orthodoxy, there is a paradoxical situation whereby one of the most ostensibly hierarchical Christian traditions is, for all intents and purposes, one of the least well defined in the United States in terms of clear ecclesial ordering and, by extension, political theologies

---

7. Cf. Herbel, *Turning to Tradition*, esp. 130ff.

of social ordering. In fact, there simply is no separating of questions of church authority and political authority in Orthodoxy, either globally or in the United States. The political is theological and vice versa. Which means that Orthodox in the United States have a wide canvas for theologizing visions of order that touch on both sacred and secular realities.

In the case of Death to the World, this canvas has been a place for it to turn its lens of rebellion upon political issues that land themselves to being emplotted within the apocalyptic frame inherited from Rose. This leads to a fascinating and complicated interweaving of issues such as communism, Russia, monarchy, New World Order, and antichrist. My goal in this chapter is to demonstrate the theo-logic that orders and renders intelligible the connections among these diverse topics.

We should note that, because Death to the World involves a number of contributors, it would be misleading to ascribe to it one unified political frame or viewpoint; however, as I hope to make clear, the broad outlines of the connections that I will try to make in this chapter are consistent and discernible throughout the movement's published writings and images.

Cosmic Authority, Cosmic Chaos

In a worldview such as that of Rose in which Marxism, particularly in its violent Bolshevik manifestations in the twentieth century,[8] is a key steppingstone to the advent of the globalist New World Order and thus the antichrist, it is not surprising that the Romanov family as a whole and Tsar Nicholas II (canonized in 1981) in particular are revered. The Romanov family is collectively sanctified on a number of Russian Orthodox calendars, and a number of saints associated with it—for instance Elizabeth the New Martyr—are both inspiring in their own right and emblematic of the vast numbers of Christians estimated to have suffered persecution and martyrdom under the Bolsheviks. The living memory of "catacomb saints" is powerful within US piety as well as Russia, in no little part due to *The Orthodox Word* and *Death to the World* highlighting their stories over decades.

The theological centrality of Tsarist monarchy endorsed by a number of Death to the World strands shows that, in the case of this movement, the "rebellion" against authority is specific: it is rebellion against the forces of government and

---

8. Rose's critique of Marx relates both to his philosophy and to the outworking of it in revolution and repression. While this might seem a characteristically "right wing" take on Marx, it is worth noting that a number of more sympathetic readers of Marx regard the Leninist/Stalinist move to enact "socialism in one country" as opposed to emphasizing international worker solidarity was indeed a recipe for totalitarian disaster. Cf. for instance Bhaskar Sunkara, *The Socialist Manifesto: The Case for Radical Politics in an Era of Extreme Inequality* (New York: Basic Books, 2019).

nihilistic or totalitarian culture that are consistent with the advent of globalization and New World Order (and thus antichrist),[9] but it also elevates authority that is strong and faithful enough to stave off (however temporarily) these currents. This is further evidence for a core thesis of this book: that the Death to the World movement has an agenda of transformation and not just appropriation of punk culture. Punk in and of itself, in this view, is rebellion for rebellion's sake but with no clear telos. Individual and collective soul transformation, meanwhile, entails rejecting the wrong authorities but embracing the right ones.

Much of the theological importance of Tsarism within Death to the World's aesthetic can be tied to invocations of the "katechon" (τὸ κατέχον), or the strongman, as the "one who withholds," as in 2 Thessalonians 2:1-7 (NRSV):

> As to the coming of our Lord Jesus Christ and our being gathered together to him, we beg you, brothers and sisters, not to be quickly shaken in mind or alarmed, either by spirit or by word or by letter, as though from us to the effect that the day of the Lord is already here. Let no one deceive you in any way; for that day will not come unless the rebellion comes first and the lawless one is revealed, the one destined for destruction. He opposes and exalts himself above every so-called god or object of worship, so that he takes his seat in the temple of God, declaring himself to be God. Do you not remember that I told you these things when I was still with you? And you know what is now restraining him [*katechon, gender neutral*], so that he may be revealed when his time comes. For the mystery of lawlessness is already at work, but only until the one who now restrains [*katechon, masculine*] is removed. And then the lawless one will be revealed, whom the Lord Jesus will destroy with the breath of his mouth, annihilating him by the manifestation of his coming.

Who is the katechon? Within much Russian Orthodox-influenced theology, it is the tsar—the cosmically ordained monarch—who restrains disorder. Moreover, in recent centuries this disorder has increasingly become linked with Marxism/communism.

Unsurprisingly for a zine that is notable for lifting up saints and martyrs persecuted under Bolshevism and Soviet Russia, the particular choice of the tsar as one who holds back Bolshevist and communists currents is important. Rose, too, understood communism as a stage in globalism/New World Order that would prepare the way for the Antichrist. In an article from the web zine, the American priest and blogger Fr. Zechariah Lynch begins by arguing that the institution of Tsarhood (the monarch) is a God-ordained truth. Unlike some American

---

9. Contemporary Orthodox writings emphasizing this, often in direct citation of Rose, are numerous. Cf. *inter alia* Father Spyridon Bailey, *Orthodoxy and the Kingdom of Satan* (FeedaReed.com, 2017) and G. M. Davis, *Antichrist: The Fulfillment of Globalization* (Jordanville, NY: Uncut Mountain Press, 2022).

Orthodox he stops short of fully condemning democracy, but he clearly asserts its inferiority to a more integrated (in Russian Orthodoxy, "symphonic") allegiance between the Church and a God-ordained monarch:

> The modern secular ideal of government is based on "Enlightenment" ideology and its subsequent evolution into the revolutionary mindset. The Granddad of modern revolutions, the French Revolution, made no attempt to hide the fact that it desired the complete overthrow of "throne and altar." The brutal history of bloody secular revolutions has always set as primary targets royalty and clergy (and anyone who would support them). A very enticing motto was created—rule for the people and by the people. The essential problem here is an inversion of authority. In the Christian ideal authority to rule (as Tsar or President) comes ultimately from God. In modern democracies the authority to rule is said to reside in, that is, takes its source from, the people. The people may choose who and what they want to rule over them (while at times, in some instances, giving lip service to God). This is pure humanism. (Democracy is not de facto bad, but the complete secular implementation of it is very faulty.) The people are deluded into thinking that they are the *source* of authority for those who rule over them; thus ascribing to themselves, as if possible, an authority that belongs to God alone. And the rulers are "freed" from the notion that they will answer to a Higher Authority and thus they now may do whatever is "right in their own eyes."[10]

Having established the theological grounding for this monarchism, Lynch uses the occasion of the Tsar's martyrdom at the hands of the Bolsheviks to render an apocalyptic vision drawing explicitly upon 2 Thessalonians:

> Thus, the Tsar stood as an icon of the reality of heavenly rule; a reminder to even other rulers of the earth that true sovereignty belongs to God Most-High, the High King of all. The Orthodox Tsar (Byzantine and Russian) is also seen as a restraining force to social chaos, lawlessness, and degeneracy. St. Paul states in 2 Thessalonians, "For the mystery of lawlessness already is energizing itself, only there is the one who restrains now, until he should be taken out of the midst. And then the lawless one shall be revealed … " (2:7–8a). "The one who restrains" is traditionally understood to be the Orthodox Tsar. St. John Chrysostom comments, "That is, whenever the empire is taken out of the way, then he shall come. For as long as there is fear of the empire, no one will willingly exalt himself. But when it is dissolved, he will attack the anarchy, and endeavor to seize upon the sovereignty both of man and God." The clear implications, in which we possibly live, are that once the Orthodox Tsar together with the Empire falls,

---

10. Zechariah Lynch, "The Cosmic Significance of Tsar Nicholas II," *Death to the World*, July 17, 2020, accessed at https://deathtotheworld.com/articles/the-cosmic-significance-of-tsar-nicholas-ii/.

then the way will be cleared for the antichrist. He will exploit the social, moral, and spiritual confusion and lawlessness which will be the dominant situation in the world ... Thus, the removal and martyrdom of the last Orthodox Tsar have vast cosmic ramifications.[11]

Lynch goes on to make the explicit connection to Marxism in the US context, albeit one in which political content has been subtly transmuted into a more spiritual register:

> Maybe the world was no longer worthy of such an ideal. Maybe we all love our own authority a little too much. Regardless, after the martyrdom of the Tsar, the world entered into a time of unheard of global chaos, socially and morally. The foundations of the "old world" have been relentlessly assaulted. A new world is indeed arising but I am afraid its end has long been prophesied. Godless, anarchist, and iconoclastic secular humanism, under the manifestation of Soviet communism, ruthlessly murdered the Tsar and his family because he was an Orthodox Christian and the Tsar. He stood as an icon of Godly rule; a reminder that humanity and all its earthly authority must answer to God ... *May those westerners with sanity hear and tremble, the godless agenda which wore the mask of sovietism is alive and well in the West.* Its mask may have had an upgrade, but the demonic face behind it remains the same.[12] [emphasis added]

I quote this Death to the World article at length, not only because it exemplifies the apocalyptic "katechon" dimension that I have been describing, but because this feature is also characteristic of a particularly American Russophile move to ascribe the role of the katechon prophetically to the Tsar, the Russian ruler, over and against the forces of decadence which are specifically identified as the West.

This theo-politics has roots in Rose himself, who works from a similar frame in his aforementioned apocalypticism:

> In the Christian apocalyptic view, we can see that the power which until now has restrained the final and most terrible manifestation of demonic activity on earth has been taken away (II Thess. 2:7), Orthodox Christian government and public order (whose chief representative on earth was the Orthodox emperor) and the Orthodox Christian world view no longer exist as a whole, and Satan has been "loosed out of his prison," where he was kept by the grace of the Church of Christ, in order to "deceive the nations" (Apoc. 20:7-8) and prepare them to worship Antichrist at the end of the age. Perhaps never since the beginning of the Christian era have demons appeared so openly and extensively as today.[13]

---

11. Ibid.
12. Ibid.
13. Rose, *Orthodoxy and the Religion of the Future* (Platina, CA: St. Herman of Alaska Brotherhood Press, 1975), 109.

Consequently, "Holy Rus," the notion that Russia has a spiritual destiny to stave off decadence and maintain Orthodoxy's vitality in the world, and to do so in such a way that its experience battling Bolshevism will give it wisdom in resisting the New World Order forces of Antichrist, has been a growing and effective ideology both in Russia and in the United States.[14] We can note, too, as have many observers, that this narrative of Tsarist providence over and against Western decadence has also played a significant role in Russia's justification for military action in the Ukraine. Needless to say, the impact of this worldview in current geopolitical events regarding Russia's aggression toward Ukraine is potentially quite significant.[15]

As mentioned above, in the case of Death to the World, this theologizing of the need for proper theo-political authority to help the faithful spiritually resist "Bolshevism" in all its political, cultural, and spiritual guises finds application in a number of areas, but nowhere more deeply than the global government response (and US domestic response) to the Covid-19 crisis. It is here that we will see how the apocalyptic backdrop of much of Death to the World's deployment of tsarism and anti-Marxism fuels a very specific—and theologically fraught—response to a global crisis.

Covid-19 and Closure

As I stated many a time, the fundamental goal of Covid-19ism (yes there was a real virus, I'm speaking of the utilizing of the virus for an agenda) was primarily psychological—masks, lockdowns (applied, eased, and applied again), new social habits, and so forth. It is also why the threat of some new disease is ever in the mainstream media. Covid-19ism proved that people, even Christians, are willing to accept a "new normal" under the threat of illness. It was priming the pump. People are willing to accept new standards of human interaction (or lack thereof) and even Christians are willing to accept the modification of worship and interaction with the Divine under the threat of an illness. Some Christians even refused the non-masked entrance into church buildings; some even willingly segregated the unvaccinated or barred them from worship. Those who would not accept the new mass psychosis were many times cut off, even by those counted as friends. What do such actions say, and have we repented and reconciled? Or has it just been easier to brush it under the carpet? Does this not indicate the danger, and on some level the potency, of what is being addressed in this article? Although it may seem at current that Covid-19ism is

---

14. Cf. John P. Burgess, *Holy Rus': The Rebirth of Orthodoxy in the New Russia* (Oxford: Oxford University Press, 2017) as well as Riccardi-Swartz, *Between Heaven and Russia*.

15. Cf. Nicholas Denysenko, *The Church's Unholy War: Russia's Invasion of Ukraine and Orthodoxy* (Eugene, OR: Cascade, 2023).

dormant, I bring it up because substantial ground was taken, through it, in the reconditioning of humanity. Certain mentalities were cultivated in many and are all still there.[16]

This recent (2022) post from the Death to the World zine, while more measured than those Orthodox who regard Covid-19 itself as a myth or a fully engineered government conspiracy, nonetheless makes clear the zine's sympathies for those who regard the response to the virus, if not the virus itself, as sinister.[17] Why might this be?

The notion that the government will seize upon chaos (either real or government-manufactured) in order to put in procedures of mass population control, as a precursor to New World order, is a mainstay of New World Order-fearing discourse and has been for quite a while. Within Orthodoxy, many US Orthodox point to the prophecies of Saint Paisios of the Holy Mountain, a saint also featured often in *Death to the World*, as prescient evidence that Covid-19 measures represent a building block toward the New World Order. The elder prophesied that a global credit system (tied, in his case, to "Zionism") would emerge as a particular collusion between communists, globalists, and the antichrist.[18] It should

---

16. Fr. Zechariah Lynch, "Sinister Psychosis and the Remembrance of God," accessed May 29, 2023, https://deathtotheworld.com/articles/sinister-psychosis-and-the-remembrance-of-god/.

17. It should be noted that Fr. Turbo Qualls, discussed in Chapter 4 as part of the revival of Death to the World, has expressed similar sentiments regarding Covid-19 and government/antichrist conspiracy; cf. Johnson, "It Takes Humility to Understand What's Happening."

18. St. Paisios' rhetoric is worth experiencing:

"It's possible that you'll live through much which is described in the Book of Revelations. Much is coming to the surface, little by little. The situation is horrible. Madness has gone beyond all bounds. Apostasy is upon us, and now the only thing left is for the 'son of perdition' (2 Thess. 2:3) to come.

The world has turned into a madhouse. A great confusion will reign, in which each government will begin to do whatever comes into its head. We'll see how the most unlikely, the most insane, events will happen. The only good thing is that these events will happen in very quick succession.

Ecumenism, common markets, a one-world government, a single made-to-order religion: such is the plan of these devils. The Zionists are already preparing their messiah. For them the false-messiah will be king, will rule here, on earth.

A great discord will arise. In this discord everyone will clamor for a king to save them. At that moment they'll offer up their man, who'll say: 'I'm the Imam, I'm the fifth Buddha, I'm the Christ whom Christians are awaiting. I'm the one whom the Jehovah's Witnesses have been waiting for. I'm the Jewish messiah.'

Difficult times are ahead. Great trials await us. Christians will suffer great persecutions. Meanwhile, it's obvious that people don't understand that we're on the verge of the end times, that the seal of the Antichrist is becoming a reality. As if nothing's happening. That's why Holy Scripture says that even the chosen will be deceived.

be noted, however, that similar concerns about the growth of global surveillance infrastructure as collusion between governments and private industry have also been articulated by philosophers and voices more associated with the political or even radical left, such as Giorgio Agamben and Byung-Chul Han.[19]

In the case of Covid-19 closures and Death to the World, once California mandated in 2020 that public gatherings must be limited and thus restricted religious gatherings, the zine on its Facebook page began to publish a variety of images parodying what it saw as the hypocrisy of allowing, as the page put it,

The Zionists want to rule the earth. To achieve their ends they use black magic and satanism. They regard Satan-worship as a means to gain the strength they need to carry out their plans. They want to rule the earth using satanic power. God is not something they take into account.

One sign that the fulfillment of prophecy is near will be the destruction of the Mosque of Omar in Jerusalem. They'll destroy it in order to restore the Temple of Solomon which used to be on the same place. In the end the Jews will pronounce the Antichrist messiah in this rebuilt temple.

The rabbis know that the true Messiah has already come and that they crucified Him. They know this, and yet they are blinded by egoism and fanaticism.

Two thousand years ago it was written in the Book of Revelations that people will be marked with the number '666'. As Holy Scripture says, the ancient Hebrews laid a tax on the peoples they conquered in various wars. The yearly tax was equal to 666 talents of gold. (3 Kings 10:14, 2 Chronicles 9:13.) Today, in order to subjugate the whole world they'll once again introduce the old tax number linked to their glorious past. That is, '666' is the number of mammon.

Everything is going as planned. They put the number a long time ago on credit cards. As a result, he who is not marked with the number '666' will be unable to buy, sell, get a loan, or find work.

Providence tells me that the Antichrist wants to subjugate the world using this system. It will be foisted upon people with the help of the mechanisms which control the world economy, for only those who receive the mark, an image with the number '666', will be able to take part in economic life.

The mark will be an image which will first be placed on all products, and then people will be compelled to wear it on their hand or forehead. Little by little, after the introduction of ID cards with the three sixes, after the creation of a personal dossier, they'll use cunning to introduce the mark.

In Brussels a whole palace with three sixes has been built to house a central computer. This computer can keep track of billions of people. And we Orthodox are resisting this because we don't want the Antichrist and we don't want dictatorship either."

19. Cf. Guillermo Andres Duque Dilva and Cristina Del Prado Higuera, "Political Theology and Covid-19: Agamben's Critique of Science as a New 'Pandemic Religion,'" *Open Theology* 7, no. 1 (October 5, 2021) and Carmen Siguenza and Esther Robello, "Byun-Chul Han: Covid-19 Has Reduced Us to a 'Society of Survival,'" *Eruactiv*, May 24, 2020, https://www.euractiv.com/section/global-europe/interview/byung-chul-han-covid-19-has-reduced-us-to-a-society-of-survival/.

"pot shops and strip clubs" to remain open, but not churches. However, as usual for Death to the World, the rebellion against the authority of one sector (the government) was paired with a reminder as to the importance of obedience and fidelity to another sector: the church. Borrowing from the language of "essential workers" allowed to operate during the pandemic, these images declare priest consecrating the elements to be "essential scientists," the holy mysteries "essential immunity," and the priest giving confession as "essential physicians," even as other images decried the silencing of these same priests by means of the bans.

To understand some of the intensity of this negative energy as well as the sacramental theology operative, it is helpful to remember that during the height of the pandemic a number of Orthodox parishes (like other Christian assemblies) broadcasted their services for those confined to their homes; however, like Roman Catholics and unlike many forms of Protestantism, Orthodox could not instigate "online" or at-home blessing of sacraments (such as communion). Liturgical assembly is central to Orthodox piety; while the church has a rich array of home-based prayer services, the in-person Divine Liturgy on Sunday morning is the sole place for the mysteries to be celebrated in their full integrity (apart from other designated in-person liturgies throughout the week and in special commemoration, all of which were also restricted during this time). Thus, the sacramental reception of most Orthodox was disrupted during the height of the pandemic amidst government restrictions.

We can also see, however, how easily one can emplot these government moves within the aforementioned narrative whereby government control of citizens (redolent of Marxism) restricts religion (evocative of Bolshevism) as a stage in consolidation of power (shades of New World Order) as a waystation to the coming of the antichrist. If one were to ponder why Death to the World seized on this Covid-19 moment so vehemently, a plausible theory is that it was almost inevitable given the sort of theo-political backdrop provided by the particular apocalyptic declension narratives that we have been describing. When one is spiritually fed over time by the powerful witness of the Russian "catacomb" saints and martyrs under horrific government repression, then it is unlikely that, even despite government citations of science and the need to preserve the health of the vulnerable, any real trust in that authority could supersede the suspicion of a government willing to close churches to achieve that goal. Our worldmaking hinges on the material we feed our minds and spirits, and worldmaking is powerful.

It would be a mistake too to regard this worldmaking as purely political and not theological. Indeed, in the case of Death to the World's repeated invocation of modern saints who suffer under Soviet/communist regimes, we can see these as critical links between the recognized saints of the past and the modern saints—and thus an enactment of the notion that sainthood is not simply something that belongs in the past, but is an injunction toward striving for holiness in the present. Consider the following article from a 2023 edition of the zine, which is an excerpt of the contemporary spiritual text *Viata parintelui Iustin Pirvu*:

We stayed with Fr. Ilie Lacatusu (†1983) four years in Periprava at the Danube Delta.

He was greatly distinguished for his internal strength and silence. Rarely did you hear him speak, and when you did he had something important to say. Frequently he exhorted us to pray when we were in a dangerous situation. This man, I must say, was truly humble. He never wanted to come to the surface, but always tried to remain unnoticed.

I remember a miraculous event that took place at the Danube Delta, in which Fr. Ilie played a significant role. On January 30th they sent us to the channel to cut bladderworts. Do you understand what this means in the middle of winter? Certain death. We were further dismayed by the fact that the guards had four guns with them. Maybe they wanted to execute us, believing that we will refuse to execute the order.

There was an opening there in the water around forty hectares, and the bladderworts were beyond deep. Everyone started telling each other that they will not enter the water. They ordered us to go in and gather two sets.

For whom were we doing this? It was without purpose. How could you enter the water? If you step into the swamp, who will pull you out? At first, we hesitated. Then Fr. Ilie decided to encourage us, saying: "Enter, because they are having bad thoughts. They will shoot us. Enter and the Panagia with the Three Hierarchs will get us out unharmed and sound."

We entered. The water reached up to our chins. We worked as if we were on dry land. For others the water was up to their necks, while others to their chest, and others to their midsection, whatever it happened to be for each of us. We were in the water for three hours and nicely brought out what they asked from us, tidy and of the same size. The temperature was -30 below and the ice had a thickness of 20 centimeters. Yellow blooming water lilies could be seen under the ice. A great miracle happened that day. That morning it was foggy, the sky was cloudy and the cold pierced your bones. Suddenly the sun came out. There came such a warmth that even the guards were surprised. We took our clothes off to dry them, and it was like we put them on the warmest stove, as the vapors came out. We dressed and returned to the prison.

Thus the Panagia and the Three Hierarchs were with us and helped us on that icy thirtieth day of January. Nobody got sick. If it wasn't for the prayers of Fr. Ilie, we would all have died.[20]

The political backdrop of this story is, again, Bolshevik persecution in Romania, and the zine choosing to excerpt it clearly serves as a not-so-subtle broadside

---

20. Iustin Parvu, "Enter," *Viata parintelui Iustin Pirvu*, trans. John Sanidopoulos, reprinted in *Death to the World* 28, (January 29, 2023), https://deathtotheworld.com/articles/enter/.

against the sort of cognate perceived persecutions of the church that we have been discussing. That said, the fact that the fundamental genre is hagiography, saint stories highlighting miracles stemming from personal piety, is significant. From a literary and theological standpoint, this move represents a sort of irruption of hagiographic trope amidst grimly modern circumstances, and the effect is resolutely theological: God still creates saints today, especially in circumstances of persecution, and thus we are all expected to strive for holiness without limit. The saints are our contemporaries, and thus our mandates. To be clear, my point here is not that these gestures are not *also* political; it is rather to highlight yet another instance where the lines between what is spiritual and what is political are blurred to the point of inextricability.

Moreover, we also see here another sort of outworking (consistent in its own way) of Death to the World's "otherworldliness." Unlike some Orthodox objectors to government shutdowns during this period, for the most part Death to the World did not weigh in directly on controversies around whether it was

Figure 4.1 "Immunity." Image from Death to the World Instagram.

Figure 4.2 "Banned Not Essential." Image from Death to the World Instagram.

theologically permissible to envision that the consecrated body and blood of Christ in the mysteries might make one ill (although some that did began to employ the aforementioned #deathtotheworld hashtag on their posts); however, it was clear from the writings and posts published during this time that the zine was calling on its adherents to focus on what it understood to be "true" health (salus, salvation), which is otherworldly, rather than prioritizing worldly health by holding back from assembly and reception of communion. In other words, what is operative here is less a miraculous view of the invulnerability to physical disease conveyed by the sacraments (although during the time Death to the World did highlight the moving hagiography of St. Nikephoros the Leper, to whom some faithful ascribed Covid-19 cures) and more an assertion that physical health, while not unimportant, is subsidiary to the spiritual health available in obedience to the church and reception of its sacraments in defiance to authorities. This is how otherworldliness gets operationalized, with very high stakes (see Figure 4.1).

Conspiracy or Prophecy?

It would be possible to look at this operationalization of Rose's apocalyptic narrative and see it as an instance of religion interacting with conspiracy theory. By "conspiracy theory," we can follow the definitions offered by sociologists Joseph E. Uscinski and Joseph Parent:

> A conspiracy is a secret arrangement between two or more actors to usurp political or economic power, violate established rights, hoard vital secrets, or unlawfully alter government institutions, and a conspiracy theory is a proposed explanation of historical, ongoing, or future events that cites as a main causal factor a small group of powerful persons, the conspirators, acting in secret for their own benefit against the common good.[21]

The distinction is important because, while a conspiracy might be a kind of public action, conspiracy theory is a mode of public discourse and reasoning that both exemplifies and impacts collective social epistemologies.

Whether or not one is inclined to see it as conspiracy theory goes back to my comments about the Rorschach test: as with any conspiracy theory, if one believes the premises of the official story as well as the authorities promulgating it, then conspiracy is crazy. If one does not, it is plausible. A theological judgment about apocalyptic declension narratives is necessary here, and how one comes down on that will very much determine how one views both the theological assertions undergirding Death to the World's interventions into politics and the particular results of those assertions in action.

In the case of Death to the World, a number of interpretive lenses are plausible, and at the end of the day much comes down to whether one is theologically inclined to discern the world according to a declension narrative (the world getting worse and worse), and a decline that follows the gathering forces of antichrist via the New World Order (as well as whether one is inclined to view such ideologies as Marxism as components of that New World Order). It is, in theory, not impossible that one could have sympathy for this apocalyptic frame and still be convinced that Death to the World stokes "conspiracy theory" on the definitions offered above; likewise, many Orthodox Christians might demur from reading history through the lenses offered by Rose and St. Paisios and would thus be even more inclined to regard Death to the World's interventions as conspiracy theorizing. Christians engaging the same premises might come to very different conclusions based on how they are arranged and emplotted, as we have been seeing.

In addition to the "essential/non-essential" workers posting, Death to the World posted (in July 2020) a collage featuring a panoply of images (see Figure 4.3).

---

21. Joseph E. Uscinski and Joseph Parent, *American Conspiracy Theories* (Oxford: Oxford University Press, 2014), 31–2.

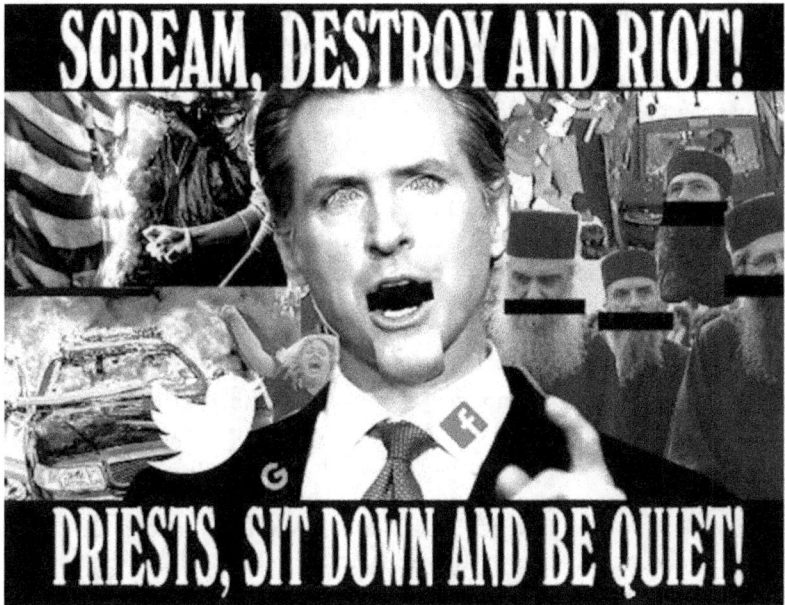

Figure 4.3 "Scream Destroy Riot." Image from Death to the World Instagram.

Centrally, California governor Gavin Newsome (who had ordered the various Covid-19 lockdowns) is portrayed with a puppet mouth and Silicon Valley logos (Facebook, Google, Twitter) on his lapels; presumably, "government as corporate puppet" is the takeaway. Priests are once again shown with censor tape, and a host of rioters (burning cars in two cases and the American flag in another) make up the backdrop. The allegation is that the governor is a hypocrite for closing churches while protests (which at the time centered around police brutality toward African Americans) were not subject to government shutdown.

For those used to receiving primarily "spiritual" content from Death to the World, such images could only be jarring. Questions around whether the protests in 2020 were actually endemically violent or whether that was a conservative media talking point press the credibility of the backdrop, and the New World Order-style rendition of a specific American politician was a significant departure from icons of saints. However, understanding this moment as one within Death to the World's ongoing outworking of the apocalyptic linkage of New World Order and Antichrist characteristic of Rose, St. Paisios, and other Orthodox figures promoted by Death to the World gives context for why this move might not have been understood as a departure from Death to the World's normal concerns by its creators.

The image provoked enough social media backlash on the Death to the World public Facebook page that the administrators (presumably Valadez) finally felt compelled to weigh in on its decision to depict the Covid-19 controversy:

> Since many commenters are assuming, we will make it very clear (again). Firstly, nowhere in this post incites riot, but presents a reality that is just as real as a thousand years ago, six months ago, or today. Yes, we have used provocative language in co-opting medical terms (which we will discuss), and that is the point. If you have been reading what we have been posting since this pandemic initially began, you would be aware that the only "rising up" we ask anyone to do is through prayer and repentance. It is us who have closed the churches by our blemished sacrifices we have offered in them and this is the spirit we must maintain. On the same side of that coin, we need to break away from the world's narrative and rush for the physical cure to this virus. While physical cures can be good if used with good stewardship, we have seen Orthodox social media become obsessed with the political and social motives behind our pandemic. We are not in our churches, not in front of the holiest things, and the internet is spooning out to us something that is (many times) alien to our spiritual life. So, it is healthy to remember where our true health comes from.[22]

The post goes on to distance Death to the World from the view that one cannot be made sick in church; however, it reiterates (as discussed above) that the deeper "cure" for the ailments that matter—mind, body, and soul—are to be found in the church's sacraments. This post exemplifies, I would argue, the tense state that the Death to the World project finds itself in—how can one maintain a focus on otherworldliness (the "diseases" and "cures" that really matter) while also intervening in highly politicized worldly conflicts?

Energy, Authority, Obedience

As I hope this chapter has made clear, it should not be fully surprising that a movement whose theo-political framework has sought (as did Rose) to continually lift up the witness of Russian Christians during the Soviet era would be primed to view government restriction of worship as a conflict within which the church's own spiritual vitality and mission were being threatened.

There is much that is concerning about the political outworking of Death to the World's theo-political aesthetic in recent years that I have been discussing in this chapter. As I will argue in the next chapter, I hold the view that the particulars of how otherworldliness is operationalized do matter both politically and spiritually, and for my part I view the Death to the World movement as stronger when it avoids being drawn into these political rabbit holes (even as we have also seen that, within the apocalyptic spiritual framework in question, that is sometimes easier said than done even on theological terms). However, my goal in this chapter has been less

---

22. Death to the World, "A Lot of Speculation," Facebook, April 30, 2020, https://www.facebook.com/DTTWzine/posts/pfbid02tr3HGbQW4HaRKa8cZVRAQFjxFA52ECjEnVq36R7UZGdaa1hmpwQbVhB4dK5FzZZTl.

to offer normative assessment of these political moves within the movement and more to show how they make sense once viewed as particular modes of narration of apocalyptic declension that are inaugurated by Rose, supported by saints such as St. Paisios, and consistent throughout Death to the World's theology. In other words, it's less about whether the moves are "right" or "wrong" and more about whether they are consistent, and the answer to the latter is, I believe, yes—even as we might envision the same otherworldliness going other ways.

This is by no means to diminish the damage that the movement is risking. As many of the scholars of conspiracy theory already cited in this chapter have shown, belief in conspiracy theory has played a major role in contemporary political violence (the January 6th, 2021 assault on the US capitol being one prominent example); moreover, to use spiritual authority to discredit potentially life-saving vaccinations without correspondingly rigorous scientific rationales is problematic in the extreme. As a citizen and as an Orthodox Christian myself, I join with many others to distance myself from these aspects of the Death to the World movement, as well as others — including intense focus on the coming "New World Order" — that seem to draw vitality less from theology and more from conspiratorial political discourse. Whether or not these more recent forays into politics are a feature or bug of the movement in its "essence" — to the extent that such an essence exists and is discernible — is a serious matter, and one that must ultimately come down to individual judgment. As I will make clear in the concluding chapter, my hope is that the answer is that these more recent trends toward explicit political engagement as fuelled by conspiracy theory are anomalous and not essential, but that is indeed a hope and not a certainty.

I want to conclude this chapter, in this spirit of the book, by pointing out how these contestations too parallel to some extent ongoing debates especially within punk rock culture. As noted above, an ethos of rebellious energy and suspicion of authority has long been a hallmark of punk rock culture; indeed, as noted above, especially in the "straight edge" punk scenes that were most directly influential on Marler, the goal of abstaining from mind-numbing drugs and behavior was to retain focused energy for resistance to the status quo that sought to push those behaviors to narcotize the population and render it docile. That said, this raises questions around how to channel that energy when it comes to politics (as ongoing conflicts over, say, skinhead punk promotion of white supremacist movements makes clear[23]). In other words, punk (and here we might sociologically demur from Death to the World's theological assessment of the subculture) has never just been raw, undirected rebellious energy. It has participated in the same contestations around authority and its "construction and corrosion" (to use Bruce Lincoln's aforementioned felicitous term[24]), as have religious movements like Death to the World. What to tear down? What to build in its place? Whom to trust? These questions are shared between punk subcultures and Orthodox

---

23. Cf. Duncombe and Tremblay, *White Riot*.
24. Lincoln, *Authority*.

cultures. From Pussy Riot storming Orthodox churches in Moscow to protest Putin's policies to anarcho-dance-punk band The KLF burning money onstage at British award shows, punk and politics has been a complex symbolic realm of fraught contestations and unstable alliances, and of course the history of religions shows the same.

At the risk of being even more abstract: both religion and art are not simply the production and promulgation of meaning that stands or falls on its own unaided merit; they are also agoras in which the proclamation of truth and meaning is adjudicated, and this adjudication is often regulated by the marketplace of appropriation by consumption. Needless to say, in such a marketplace authority questions—who gets to decide—are part of what is being worked out, and the outworking of these questions is not always reducible to politics, but it is also never apart from them.[25] This sociological fact, to be sure, does not in and of itself decide whether any given pronouncement (be it theological praise of Tsar Nicholas II in a zine or a punk protest against the G8 summit) is true or false; as Paul shows us, cosmic truth as well as falsehood can both be spoken in the marketplace (Acts 17:16-24). But it does mean that, as much as many Death to the World fans might wish for more or less melding of spirituality and politics (depending on their tastes in both), under the conditions of apocalyptic anti-modern discourse the lines between them are not always easy to draw—even if it continues to matter that they be sketched and walked well, and with discernment.

---

25. Cf. Saler, *Between Magisterium and Marketplace*.

Chapter 5

THEOLOGICAL POTENTIAL(S)

The previous chapters have attempted to show how Death to the World, as well as the various movements that cite it as direct inspiration or share in key aspects of its theo-aesthetics, operates at the intersection of longstanding and pressing issues of theology, politics, and authority within contemporary US Orthodoxy. Moreover, I have argued that these productive tensions parallel, and in some cases are helpfully brought into dialogue with, similar debates and navigations within punk rock culture(s).

In this chapter, we can sharpen our inquiry in a specifically theological direction and ask: how can a theology that takes the frame of Death to the World as its apocalyptic orientation helpfully advance those aspects of the movement that are theologically salutary—rebellion against nihilism and its cultural outworking, harnessing of countercultural energy in a disciplined direction, rigorous refusal to conflate spiritual progress with bourgeois contemporary mores—while tacking away from what I have argued are some problematic temptations within the movement as it stands (namely, an overfocus on immanent politics and conspiracy thinking)? I offer these reflections less in the spirit of telling Death to the World's creators and curators what they ought to do—which would hardly be very punk rock of me!—and more as a testimony as to how this theological scholar continues to value the theo-aesthetics of the movement.

I will focus on three theological debates in which I think the Death to the World movement, as described in the previous chapters, can helpfully intervene: the relationship between deconstructive theology and law, the ethics and aesthetics of commodified religious images, and the epistemological differences between theology and conspiracy theory.

The Bodies That Law Creates

Christians considering how "death" might carry salvific overtones may naturally gravitate toward Paul's description in Romans of the shape of the baptismal life as "dying and rising with Christ," specifically Romans 6:3-11 (NRSV):

> Do you not know that all of us who have been baptized into Christ Jesus were baptized into his death? Therefore we have been buried with him by baptism

into death, so that, just as Christ was raised from the dead by the glory of the Father, so we too might walk in newness of life. For if we have been united with him in a death like his, we will certainly be united with him in a resurrection like his. We know that our old self was crucified with him so that the body of sin might be destroyed, and we might no longer be enslaved to sin. For whoever has died is freed from sin. But if we have died with Christ, we believe that we will also live with him. We know that Christ, being raised from the dead, will never die again; death no longer has dominion over him. The death he died, he died to sin, once for all; but the life he lives, he lives to God. So you also must consider yourselves dead to sin and alive to God in Christ Jesus.

As a number of scholars have pointed out,[1] Romans 5–6 contain a striking shift in its central soteriological imagery midway through Paul's explication of justification. While Romans 5 offers images that are consistent with a "forensic" understanding of justification—that is, believers in Christ being adjudged righteous within the framework of God as just judge—Paul somewhat abruptly shifts to the above visceral images of death and life: believers literally joining Christ in death and resurrection by God's grace.

What might account for this shift? It is generally accepted within contemporary Pauline scholarship that Paul's invocations of "law" generally operate on multiple levels, with regard not just to the Hebraic law which, as a Jew, he was willingly subject but also to Roman imperial law by which, as a citizen, he and many of his followers were bound.[2] Paul, far from being the sort of uncritical champion of law and authority that, say, decontextualized readings of Romans 13 might suggest, had as one of this key theological agendas proclaiming the irreducible contrasts and conflicts between the violently repressive and colonialist "Roman peace" and the peaceful reign of the crucified and risen Lamb of God, an agenda shared by many of his fellow New Testament authors.[3] Thus, it is legitimate to speculate that, against a backdrop wherein the structures of "law" were so often not capable of hosting the event of life-giving justice,[4] Paul might have been motivated in explicating the theological core of believers' salvation in Christ to change course from soteriological rhetoric that relies too heavily upon legalistic imagery.

However, as the aforementioned scholars point out, following this train of thought discloses a deeper possibility for Paul's motivation for the shift: to

---

1. Cf. especially Theodore W. Jennings Jr., *Outlaw Justice: The Messianic Politics of Paul* (Palo Alto, CA: Stanford, 2013), and Gerhard O. Forde, *Justification by Faith: A Matter of Death and Life* (Eugene, OR: Wipf and Stock, 2012).

2. Cf. Neil Elliott, *The Arrogance of Nations: Reading Romans in the Shadow of Empire* (Minneapolis: Fortress, 2008).

3. Cf. Barbara Rossing, *The Rapture Exposed: The Message of Hope in the Book of Revelation* (New York: Basic Books, 2005).

4. Cf. Theodore W. Jennings Jr., *Reading Derrida/Thinking Paul: On Justice* (Palo Alto, CA: Stanford, 2005).

expose the limits of the law and thus highlight the radical character of Christian discipleship. To see this in action we might ask: what is the law's furthest point, its limit, its eschaton, its end? In other words, what is produced at the absolute limit of what the law can do? The answer, at least within Paul's theological frame, is clear: what is found at the limits and end of the law is a dead body. The absolute eschaton of coercive law—both in the sense of its furthest extent, the absolute most that it can do, and in the sense of its function, its natural telos in a fallen world—is to kill, to regulate transgression by killing the transgressor. The Christian affirmation that "Jesus Christ is the end of the law," then, in a Pauline frame, operates on multiple levels. As the Messiah of the God of Abraham, Isaac, and Jacob, Jesus Christ is the fulfillment of the law, and as the crucified and broken criminal on the cross, Jesus Christ is the telos of imperial law.

But if law has reached its end in the executed body of Jesus of Nazareth,[5] and if, for Paul, to be baptized into Christ is to be joined in relentlessly bodily fashion to this body, then God's raising of Jesus from the dead is similarly a resurrection apart from, in excess of, the bounds of the law. It has been fashionable in the literature of so-called "emergent" churches to envision this baptized reality as akin to the condition of being a "pirate" (on the idea, whether historically accurate or apocryphal, that pirate ships would fly the skull and crossbones to signify that the sailors aboard were "dead" and thus outside the jurisdiction of maritime law[6]), and Jennings refers to this state as "outlaw justice."[7] For our purposes, we can notice the resonance between a Christianity that is not assimilable to "the law," with all its overtones of bourgeois respectability, upward mobility, and moralistic conformity and a Christianity that is regarded as dangerous precisely for apocalyptic reasons: if pirates and outlaws, then why not punks?

Fr. Valadez, in describing the punk lifestyle from which many Death to the World adherents come, often cites the chorus of the Sex Pistols track "No Future" as evidence of the nihilism that undergirds punk's rebellion[8]; however, we can note again the real strand of truth in this phrase when it is applied to "respectable" religion. When spirituality is too easily assimilated into "law," that is, to existing frameworks of social respectability and the coercion that enforces them, then it has "no future," no more future than the telos of the law itself. Without engaging in too much equivocation, we can say that this warning might apply to both

---

5. Cf. Mark Lewis Taylor, *The Executed God: The Way of the Cross in Lockdown America*, 2nd edition (Minneapolis, MN: Fortress Press, 2015) as well as Saler, *Theologia Crucis*.

6. Cf. Kester Brewin, *Mutiny! Why We Love Pirates and How They Can Save Us* (London: Vaux, 2016).

7. Jennings, *Outlaw Justice*.

8. As quoted in Emily Bowen, "When the Sex Pistols said, 'There is no future,' like in punk rock, there really is no future. There is no future, and that's a really depressing thing to be living for. And Orthodoxy teaches that there is a future, and it's something great to live for." "Death to the World: The Last True Rebellion," *The Outline*, December 12, 2016, https://theoutline.com/post/715/death-to-the-world.

the immanentized religious right and the immanentized left. On the right, the cooptation of Christianity to serve agendas of patriotism and idolatrous Christian nationalism in the United States may give a temporary boost of political and ecclesial energy to certain Christian coalitions, but the despair palpable in these gestures points to the fact that their long-term viability (or moral standing) in a rapidly secularizing society is doubtful.[9] Likewise, as historians such as David Hollinger have long pointed out, religion that ties its reason for existing too closely to progressive causes in a society that has, on the whole, largely assimilated these causes over the last century may achieve secular short-term victories but may eventually lose institutional vitality once those victories are won.[10] And meanwhile, a number of scholars have critiqued how easily more politically and ecclesially vague notions of "spirituality" are coopted by the relentless consumerism of late capitalism—a possibility that haunts any religiously influenced merchandising enterprise like Death to the World.[11] Put bluntly, fully immanentized religion tends to stand or fall with the apparatus of "law" upon which it stakes itself, and the results thus far are uninspiring.

Just as punk rock in the 1970s and after resisted, not necessarily calls for love and justice articulated by the various mainstream progressive movements around it but rather the domestication necessitated by playing within the rules of the "system," a genuinely punk rock theology might be an irascible and unassimilable voice within the theological scene, a voice that refuses to speak law when shouting apocalypse is more like gospel proclamation.[12] And to the extent that such a punk theology might learn specifically from Death to the World, then it might discern that a key component to this unassimilability is a sort of "out-of-time" character

---

9. Cf. Whitehead and Perry, *Taking America Back for God* and Philip S. Gorski and Samuel L. Perry, *The Flag and the Cross: White Christian Nationalism and the Threat to American Democracy* (Oxford: Oxford University Press, 2022).

10. Cf. David Hollinger, *After Tongues of Cloven Fire: Protestant Liberalism in Modern American History* (Princeton, NJ: Princeton University Press, 2013). To be clear, agreeing with the broad outlines of Hollinger's thesis does not necessitate endorsing a fully linear and determined scripted for such victories (and Hollinger operates with no such schema). As, for instance, the fate of abortion laws in the United States makes clear, there is neither linearity nor inevitability to the victory of "progressive" causes in the US context. However, the basic trends in favor of such characteristically progressive causes as gender equality, acceptance of LGBTQ+ rights, racial reconciliation, and so on are discernible in the long view.

11. Cf. *inter alia* Jeremy R. Carrette and Richard King, *Selling Spirituality: The Silent Takeover of Religion* (London: Routledge, 2004) and Jain, *Selling Yoga*.

12. Lest this seem impossibly niche or apolitical, it is worth noting that one of the signal achievements of James Cone's Black liberation theology was to self-consciously introduce apocalyptic, including God's wrath, into what he took to be a fully domesticated and toothless progressive theological milieu. Cf. especially James Cone, *God of the Oppressed* (Maryknoll, NY: Orbis, 1997).

embodied in the witness of saints and martyrs living in eras and contexts that modernity has taught us to regard as "other," irretrievable, hopelessly lost to us enlightened moderns. But what if this veil of distance is truly an illusion?

If I may be permitted a personal note: I raise that last possibility with significant trepidation. A number of excellent Eastern Orthodox theological scholars, many of whom I regard as colleagues and friends, are devoting their scholarly careers and investing significant personal energy into the task of articulating the ancient faith in terms compatible with the undeniable advances of the modern age as regards science, human rights, certain technologies, and so on; thus, my invocation of the value of "resisting the modern age" (in Death to the World's terms) is by no means meant to disparage their work or its value to the church.[13] To the extent that the Death to the World community shares Fr. Seraphim Rose's disdain for academic Orthodox systematic theology, that is not a view that I am advocating. Rather, my point is that it is quite consonant with an Orthodox academic theological frame to assert that Orthodox theology's normative view of the witness of saints and martyrs across time is in part a resistance to any theological periodization that is so linear as to make the voices of the past either unavailable or shrouded in the mist of alterity. Put more directly, a large part of the power of Death to the World (and, I believe, its ongoing theological relevance) is its aesthetic performance of the belief that our age and the age of the great martyrs and confessors have more in common than modernity or its various "posts" would have us believe. In an era of forgetfulness, it can take strong tonic to keep memory alive.

It is important to note, as articulated throughout this book, that when it comes to the punk ethos the Death to the World movement operates more in the mode of replacement than appropriation. That is, at least in the view of Marler and Valadez, a Death to the World "theology" would not so much be a "punk theology" as I am outlining it here as it would be a presentation of timeless Eastern Orthodox wisdom with an aesthetic that speaks to those formed by punk/metal subcultures. However, I am taking what I hope is a warranted liberty based on the diversity and vitality of the movement that I have been describing and suggesting that the rebellious energy of punk that Death to the World has always acknowledged, and to a certain extent admired, remains a helpful tonic within the theological scene as a whole. The timelessness of the witness of the church's saints and martyrs that Death to the World showcases disrupts the modern systems that even we theological scholars set up to mute them by making them "sources" for our theologies, in a manner perhaps akin to how the punk band Fear famously refused to be simply slotted as "entertainment" on the mainstream showcase Saturday Night Live in 1981 and in so doing changed what music on television could be.[14] To read Death to the World is to feel this chronological collapse in real time.

---

13. Cf. for instance Aristotle Papanikolaou and Elizabeth Prodromou (eds.), *Thinking through Faith: New Perspectives from Orthodox Christian Scholars* (Yonkers, NY: St. Vladimir's Seminary Press, 2008).

14. Cf. Mattson, *We're Not Here to Entertain*, esp. 62–4.

But, if this is at all true, then it also serves as a caution against the concurrent tendency within the Death to the World movement to tie the timeless witness of the saints too closely to the "signs of the times" in an immanentized political fashion. The fourth chapter of the book has been my attempt to show why it is very understandable that some of the political motifs that have increasingly become associated with Death to the World (particularly as regards critiques of "cultural Marxism," Covid-19 policy, and conspiracy theory thinking) have been so easily integrated into the sort of apocalypticism and cultural critique that the movement generates; moreover, on a purely human level, we can certainly acknowledge that the intensity of the pandemic and our age of societal divisions have not brought out the best of our political and ecclesial selves. And perhaps we can similarly acknowledge that it will be the task of future historians of this period to point out which public measures to combat the pandemic ended up being fully justified and which may have represented government overreaches, particularly as regards religious assemblies.

As suggested earlier, too, I would assert that the state-sponsored restriction and regulation of worship attendance, whether history will deem it justified or not, was particularly fraught for those shaped by Death to the World's theological and aesthetic values. Specifically, for a movement whose theo-political imagination has been so intimately impacted by the living memory within Orthodoxy of the witness of the Russian martyrs and catacomb churches during the Soviet era, and, in a very different register, the Romanovs in the face of Marxist insurrectionists, government restriction of worship was bound to awaken a resistant energy and prompt, not only an affect of persecution, but a sense that the church's own integrity was at stake in resisting.

Understandability is not inevitability, though, nor is it destiny. Again, it is not my task in this book to make specific recommendations as to where the Death to the World movement "ought" to go; as a fan and appreciative critic, though, it is my role to contextualize these recent political gestures and to express theological/aesthetics concerns about them.

To take a specific example: a recent T-shirt offering on the Death to the World site features green camouflage patterning as the backdrop to a skull (as we have seen, a common visual set piece of Death to the World) and the saying "Give me Orthodoxy or Give me Death." The phrase itself has a venerable history within Orthodoxy; for instance, a prominent monastery on Mt. Athos, a deeply holy site for global Orthodoxy, flies a black flag with a similar phrase. And the tagline has featured prominently on a number of Death to the World products. What is striking about this design, though, is the fact that the logo and skull are printed on unquestionably martial imagery (the camouflage): see Figure 5.1.

It is a bit hard to know what to make of this. On the one hand, as we have seen, "warfare" imagery (especially "spiritual" or "unseen" warfare) is central to Death to the World's theology and aesthetic, including its regard for the historic monastics (such as the desert fathers) who employ the martial framework often. Moreover, appropriation of military fashion has a venerable history within punk rock and metal countercultures as well, including straight edge. And finally, theology is no

Figure 5.1 "Orthodoxy or Death" T-shirt from Death to the World.

stranger to imagery related to "the Church Militant." However, within the context of pitched emotions and culture war energy characteristic of the contemporary era, it is hard to avoid the impression that explicitly military aesthetics coupled with "give me Orthodoxy or give me death" signals, intentionally or not, a marked theological shift from "dying for the faith" in the sense of nonviolent martyrdom (the subject of so many of the zine's hagiographies) to "dying for the faith" on a literal battlefield.

But a battle against what? Two options for opponents present themselves: human opponents and demonic ones. The struggle to the death could be against demonic spiritual forces of the Antichrist, as in Rose's theology, or the all-too-human political foes of villainized opposition: Marxism, Covid-19 policy enforcers, nonbelievers, and so on and so forth. And, sadly, the history of the faith shows that, in the heat of controversy, it is not always easy to keep the latter from being portrayed (and fought against) as the former. Put simply: how much "orthodoxy or death" might function as a multivalent invocation that allows room for applying it spiritually or politically as the situation demands, putting it against camouflage moves the aesthetic and theological energy so far in a "worldly" political direction that spiritual richness is lost: "Death to the world" risks becoming less "become as dead to the world" and more "kill the world."

Drawing from the history of punk rock, one might reasonably object here that the most vital, and indeed "timeless," punk anthems draw, not from generic rebellion, but specific historical circumstances; for instance, the Dead Kennedys' 1980 track "Holiday in Cambodia" stands as a powerful anti-imperialistic war protest even as its core imagery is drawn from the specifics of the US government-sponsored atrocities of "Operation Menu." On this logic, Death to the World's periodically focusing its antimodern rebellion against specific cultural and political targets could be seen as more effective and more transcendent of time and place, just as (to take an ecclesial parallel) hagiography derives its content-transcending power from specific details of the saints' lives and not just generalized invocations of "faithfulness" or "holiness." This objection has merit and is not easily dismissed.

In response, though, we may assert that the choice of which contemporary conflicts to thus highlight is crucial, since what is at stake from a theo-aesthetic perspective is the question of whether the dog is wagging the tail or the reverse: is the specificity of the theo-political critique serving (and being normed by) the comparative timelessness of the theological message, or is the deep reservoir of theological and spiritual power that is the Church's treasure being recruited to lend intensity and affective energy to politics? This is a question of spiritual discernment, and there is no once and for all a priori answer. But again, as a fan and critic, I would suggest that much of the spiritual power of the Death to the World movement in the future depends on how well all of its creatives and curators engage this discernment. Context in favor of embodied theological proclamation has power. Co-optation of theology for political purposes is somewhat less inspiring.

Perhaps my entire book is best conceived as a (hopefully) reasoned plea from a Death to the World fan that those who shape it be mindful of the ways in which the language of rebellion, of anti-modernity, and of the need to be mindful of the signs of the times can be deployed in ways that bring life, and those that support the forces of death. There is no a priori solution to this danger; anything that is good can be abused, and as the church teaches, abuse does not prevent right use. But, like punk rock itself, this content is volatile, and needs to be handled carefully and with love.

Clothing Resurrected Bodies

To continue by following Romans' frame, then: if outlaw Christians, if those consuming and living punk rock theology, are called to a baptismal life outside the law, outside the strictures of social responsibility and worldly upward mobility, then what does a dead and resurrected body consume? For the monks, being "dead to the world" meant wearing rags and consuming as strict a diet of food (physically) and sacred writings (spiritually) as possible; how does that square, then, with a movement centered around a website that sells content but also patches, shirts, bags, stickers?

The question is not that strange, theologically: consumption and theology have long gone hand in hand. Jesus' cooking and eating fish on the beach in John 21 stands as a testament to the "fleshliness" of his resurrection. Consuming the Eucharist has long been considered a, if not the, defining constitutive feature of the Christian life. As Kathryn Lofton has argued persuasively, practices of religion and practices of consumption are so deeply intertwined historically and in the present that any strict separation between the "spiritual" and "consumptive" realms is not only untenable but a lost opportunity for scholarly analysis.[15]

Nor is it strange within analysis of punk rock cultures: the entire question of how much subculture can engage the realm of commerce without "selling out" is a perennial one. Marler's punk rock mentor, Ian MacKaye, at one point refused to sell Fugazi merchandise on tour because of the complexity of mixing commerce and art in a way that would not damage the art's integrity; that said, merchandise ("merch") sales—especially as brokered directly between artists and fans as opposed to mediated by corporate entities—have often been the financial lifeblood of independent music and art scenes, especially in an age of digital streaming.[16] To mention the popular mall chain Hot Topic in many punk/metal circles is to conjure immediate images of corporate sellout and domesticated, commodified art;[17] however, many in those same scenes will strive to attain collectible

---

15. Lofton, *Consuming Religion*.
16. Ct. Thompson, *Punk Productions*.
17. The humorous lyrics of MC Lars' 2006 track might be taken as emblematic. A sample:
"Misfits candle tins (Are not punk rock!)
ICP throw blankets (Are not punk rock!)
Beaded Elvis curtains (Are not punk rock!)
Talking Lambchop plush dolls (Are not punk rock!)
AC/DC hair clips (Are not punk rock!)
Spongebob wristbands (Are not punk rock!)
Sex Pistols boxer shorts (Are not punk rock!)
Dischord back catalog (Okay. Maybe that's punk rock.)
Hot Topic is not punk rock! ...
Hot Topic is a contrived identification with youth subcultures to manufacture an anti-authoritarian identity and make millions. The $8 you paid for the Mudvayne poster would be better spent used to see your brother's friend's band.
DIY ethics are punk rock.
Starting your own label is punk rock.
G.G. Allin was punk rock.
But when a crass corporate vulture feeds on mass-consumer culture, this spending mommy's money is not punk rock!"

(consume-able) artifacts such as rare vinyl, shirts, zines, etc. Theologically and ideologically normed veneration of material relics is, to put it bluntly, a shared feature of Orthodox and punk rock cultures.

In this book I have noted that, from its founding by Marler to its current manifestations, the Death to the World movement has trended in more merch-heavy, material directions; more shirts, pins, flags, patches, bags, etc. (and this, perhaps ironically, as the content of the zine itself has moved more online even as the print copies remain niche options for consuming/collecting that content). This fact again presents us with several interpretive options: we could regard this move to a business/mission model where (as Fr. Valadez readily admits[18]) the sale of merchandise supports the relatively bare-bones operation of producing the zine's content as a kitschy or corporate "selling out" of some presumed "authentic" soul of the movement, or we can regard it as an aesthetically and theologically nuanced multi-platforming of the Death to the World aesthetic in a manner appropriate to a postmodern internet age *and* the persistent materiality of Orthodoxy throughout the ages. In a theological argument so integral to Orthodoxy that its imperial outworking would eventuate in the annual "Feast of the Triumph of Orthodoxy" commemoration, St. John of Damascus famously wrote concerning the materiality and image-centeredness of Orthodox piety:

> Of old, God the incorporeal and uncircumscribed was never depicted. Now, however, when God is seen clothed in flesh, and conversing with men, I make an image of the God whom I see. I do not worship matter, I worship the God of matter, who became matter for my sake, and deigned to inhabit matter, who worked out my salvation through matter. I will not cease from honouring that matter which works my salvation.[19]

To be absolutely clear, Death to the World products are not icons proper; indeed, as we have seen, a number of cognate aesthetic movements discussed in this book have followed Death to the World's lead in being reticent about (or in some cases refusing) to make wearable merchandise out of icons or saint visages proper. However, as Paul J. Griffiths has perceptively noted, sub-iconographic art (what might be called, colloquially or sometimes dismissively, as "kitsch") has and continues to be vital for sustaining the spiritual life precisely of those believers who are least likely, by choice or by finite means, to engage elite artistic production outside of temples or churches.[20] My claim is not that Death to the World is

---

18. Floridoxy, "Fr. John Valadez and Death to the World."

19. St. John of Damascus, *On Holy Images*, trans. Mary H. Allies (London: Baker, 1898), 16.

20. "Christianity—Catholic, Protestant, and Orthodox—has been and remains among the great generators of kitsch, and that is because Christianity is and always has been a religion of peasants and proles. Most Christian art is and always has been kitsch: that's what most Christians like, and they like it exactly because it has the principal identifying mark

kitsch in this direct sense any more than, say, paper reproductions of icons on a parish bulletin (which are themselves controversial in some Orthodox circles) are kitsch; however, the value of Griffiths' point is in its articulation of the historically undeniable and theologically salutary fact that spiritually beneficial Christian materiality has never operated on the same aesthetic logic as "high" or perhaps even fully "sacred" art. Functional access to Christian beauty has often consisted in tempering allegiance to what Walter Benjamin has famously identified as the "aura" of original works (such as handmade icons) and embracing the democratization of "mechanical reproducibility" as a spiritual good, not as a cheapening.[21]

We might think, too, of the ways in which saints are identified within the Orthodox church. In contrast to the more formalized procedures employed by Roman Catholicism, Orthodox recognition of sainthood, the path to visible sanctity (so demarcated because, on an Orthodox understanding, only God knows all the saints, visible and invisible) is a more organic one. In Orthodoxy, devoted iconographers, or perhaps even amateur artists, begin to image the person in question within material objects for devotion, and eventually icons with the required nimbus (halo). Hymns to the candidate (e.g., akathists) might also be composed. In the case of Death to the World, this in fact is particularly apposite since now-Blessed Father Seraphim Rose, whom I have argued is in many respects the "patron saint" of the movement, has in fact now formally been recognized as being on this very track.[22] My point in mentioning this detail is to note the appropriateness that a zine and movement designed, among other things, to make contemporary what some might consider to be the most extreme examples of sanctity in the church's memory might also be conceived as part of the Church's ongoing democratized, material collective discernment as to how God's Holy Spirit

of kitsch, which is to be free of nuance, lacking in subtlety. A kitschy artifact leaves those who interact with it in no doubt about how they should respond. The Stations of the Cross, present on the walls of every Catholic church, are not subtle and are not supposed to be. They are there to conform you to the bloody sufferings of Christ ... The connoisseur's hushed, museum-trained gaze is not well-designed for these purposes. That gaze values subtlety, complexity, ambiguity, and irony. Its most characteristic grace note is self-congratulation at being the kind of person who likes this rare and beautiful thing, whatever it may be, laced always with contempt for those too crude, too uneducated, or too simple to be able to do so." Paul Griffiths, *Decreation: The Last Things of All Creatures* (Waco, TX: Baylor, 2014), 324–5. Cf. also Betty Spackman, *A Profound Weakness: Christians and Kitsch* (Austin, TX: Piquant Press, 2005).

21. Cf. Walter Benjamin, *The Work of Art in the Age of Mechanical Reproduction*, trans. J. A. Underwood (Harlow: Penguin Books, 2008) as well as Sarah Riccardi-Swartz, "Holy Pixels: The Transformation of Eastern Orthodox Icons," in Mikhail Suslov (ed.), *Digital Orthodoxy in the Post-Soviet World* (Stuttgart: Ibidem-Verlag, 2016), 261–84.

22. Indeed, the proprietors of Punks and Monks books, discussed above, have been key American coordinators of this ecclesial canonization effort. Cf. https://orthochristian.com/148059.html.

is Christologically patterning saints and witnesses even now. If this is at all the case, it places Death to the World in a long line of faithful aesthetic groundswells on behalf of holiness within the church—some of which share its same ambiguities around the excesses that such surges can take.

This is important, too, since the flip side to worry about whether Death to the World's aesthetic is too grim or morbid is the question that haunts much Christian art, especially prominent in "Christian rock" and "Christian film" discussions: is it cheesy?[23] That is, is it so didactic when it comes to what it is trying to promote that the quality of the art ends up suffering?

To a certain extent, that is a question that those encountering the zine and its related textualities will need to discern for themselves, and at the end of the day there is no arguing over taste. I would suggest, though, that the stories of Marler, Valadez, and others engaged in creating and curating the legacy of the movement once again pattern a certain kind of movement and progression: even if not a full replacement of one subculture (punk/metal) within another (Orthodoxy), at least a clear hierarchy of goals that move one closer to the sort of truth that ultimately needs no gimmickry to prop it up. The vast majority of what one encounters in Death to the World is relatively "uncut" and sober ecclesial content, and in that sense, it is a very different phenomenon than, say, replacing the words of popular music with "J-count" Christian lyrics without changing the music, or melding pop culture and Christian culture in ways that do not presume the desirability of the soul gradually being acclimated away from the one and to the other.[24] Death to

---

23. Cf. Jay R. Howard and John R. Streck, *Apostles of Rock: The Splintered World of Contemporary Christian Music* (Lexington, MA: University Press of Kentucky, 2004) as well as Saler, *All These Things into Position*.

24. We can see this, for instance, within Death to the World in an article by Father Michael Reagan: "Perhaps the greatest tragedy of modern Christendom, besides its having divorced itself from communion with the historic, Apostolic Church, is that it imitates Cain in its stubborn refusal to be corrected by the same. Rather than answering the question of 'What is true worship?' by looking backward to see what the early Christians did, it puts a premium on devising continually 'new and contemporary' forms of worship that ultimately are geared more toward entertaining the participants and pleasing them, rather than on pleasing God. Contemporary worship must be 'exciting and lively' and 'meeting the people where they are at' rather than on holy and reverential and lifting the people up to where God is at.

The contemporary worship experience can very nearly be likened to a junkie continually seeking a new and better 'high', and the value of a morning's worship is evaluated entirely on whether or not its participants feel 'blessed' by it. Does this not indicate the self-centered nature of such an experience, that they are putting their own blessing ahead of God's? Can we imagine that St. Paul's only concern for the church in Corinth was that they 'get their socks blessed off during worship' and if they weren't, then perhaps they should replace the bass guitarist with someone more 'spirit-led'? His primary concern for them was that they judge and conduct themselves rightly in order to partake of the Body and Blood of the Lord

the World is not trying to change punk or metal; it is trying to transform the souls of punks and metalheads, and that is a very different thing.

Again, that will not be to everyone's tastes aesthetically or theologically, but it is a different project than opportunistic and didactic (and thus inherently cheesy) amalgamation. In Death to the World's conception, entering Orthodoxy by any means ultimately is an invitation to an apocalyptic soul journey, with the eschatological goal of the church's liturgical and aesthetic rhythms becoming "all in all" in Christ (1 Corinthians 15:28). This does not settle the question as to whether Death to the World sufficiently distinguishes itself from other Christian outreach projects that draw on popular/subcultural aesthetics, but it hopefully brings clarity as to what is distinct about it.

Theo-Aesthetic Epistemology: Faith Informing Reason or Conspiracy?

As mentioned above, one of the more troubling aspects of Fr. Seraphim Rose's apocalyptic worldview is its nods to global conspiracy theory, including anti-Judaism and invocations of New World Order. And we saw in the previous chapter how this legacy of Rose, combined with other cultural factors in an internet age, has indeed allowed conspiracy thinking to take significant root within the Death to the World movement. That chapter examined the social and political impact of this reality, but how can we assess it theologically?

One striking feature of many contemporary conspiracy theories (newer ones such as false flag accusations around school shootings as well as perennial themes such as New World Order) is that they tend to operate in a manner akin to many theodicies. As noted above, scholars of conspiracy theory tend to focus on how these causal explanations ascribe agency for adverse events to hidden, malign actors working to undermine the common good. Theologically, we can recognize the attractiveness of this impulse in producing the same kind of epistemological/affective reward that those theologies who ascribe all evil in life either to a fully deterministic God or, in more dualistic fashion, to an empowered demonic force with total or near-total control over the events of history. Theologian and biblical scholar Elaine Pagels has argued that, when it comes to life's tragedies (particularly "natural evil," or evil not immediately discernible as having been caused by particular historical agents), most of us would rather feel guilty than helpless.[25] It brings us comfort to believe that something or someone has control, even if that something is evil, because the alternative seems to be existential chaos. Conspiracy

---

in a worthy manner, for without this they were not providing the spiritual worship which they owed to God." Micheal Reagan, "In Spirit and Truth," *Death to the World* 13, February 2, 2013, accessed at https://deathtotheworld.com/articles/zine-articles/in-spirit-and-truth-issue-13/

25. Elaine Pagels, *Adam, Eve, and the Serpent* (New York: Penguin, 1988).

theory speaks to that economy of emotional and spiritual award. But what is the cost of this comfort?

The case of Alex Jones' "Infowars" following the tragic shootings of elementary school students at Sandy Hook Elementary School in Newtown, CN, in 2012 is a disturbing but salient case in point. Even before it became clear that a disturbed young man named Adam Lanza had, acting alone, used an automatic weapon to murder twenty-six victims (most of them children), conspiracy theories from Jones and related programs began positing either that the entire episode was a fake ("crisis actors" masquerading as bereaved parents at the behest of the government) or, even more darkly, that the government itself had orchestrated the shootings in order to create public support for gun control legislation (thus, by extension, working to disarm the general populace in anticipation of a sinister takeover of the citizenry by the New World Order government).

Put bluntly, the question at hand is not so much why an opportunist like Alex Jones would seize the chance to generate outrage (and thus profits) by promulgating this narrative; the deeper question is why so many were ready to believe it (even though Jones would later be sued successfully for libel by the families of the victims). Here again we can borrow Pagels' insight: while it is (hopefully) repugnant to most people to imagine a government so depraved as to murder citizens to advance a legislative agenda, there is a certain comfort in believing this as opposed to facing a world in which such horrific tragedies happen apart from such direct ascribable causality (particularly human agents). To say this is not, in this case, to render a theodicy-based judgment about how Christians, for instance, *should* regard the role of God, demonic powers, etc. in Sandy Hook. It is only to point out that conspiracy theories and theodicies are similarly structured so as to produce certain kinds of assurances in a world of violence and threatened chaos.[26]

To the extent that this is the case, and to the extent that Death to the World (like Rose's Orthodox Survival Course) seeks to form those who engage with it, then much is at stake in how the "enemy" (or controlling agential force) is described, and what counsel is given for responding to it. Rose's original "Orthodox Survival Courses," mentioned above, are somewhat paradoxical in that they insist that the true principalities and powers behind evil (including persecution of the faithful) are spiritual and not human; however, much of the content of the courses are devoted to all-too-human opponents: ecumenists, new age advocates, the government (including in its involvement in UFO investigations), and ultimately the New World Order. Rose may identify the real culprit as the Antichrist, but his

---

26. Fairness perhaps requires us to note here that this sort of response to tragedy is not the exclusive domain of the political Right; 9/11 "Trutherism" in both its hard forms ("the government crashed the twin towers") and softer forms ("the government knew about Al-Qaeda's plot and allowed the attack to happen") is a similarly structured theory that emerged from the Left.

Antichrist has a suspiciously human set of faces (although, as Bernard McGinn has ably demonstrated, this supernatural to human slippage is hardly new when it comes to invocations of the Antichrist[27]).

The danger here, as mentioned earlier in the discussion of Death to the World's take on apocalyptic more broadly, is that the immanentization of the apocalyptic frame feeds the desire to demonize human opponents and to do so with religious fervor appropriate to spiritual warfare. In a profound meditation on the ongoing theological vitality of the "spiritual warfare against demons" motif, Richard Beck has argued that, at its best, Christian talk of demons and the devil as supernatural entities has served as a safeguard precisely against making humans out to be demonic forces; in other words, letting the devil be the devil means that humans are not themselves the devil.[28] As just noted, however, history has rarely worked out that way: Martin Luther called the papacy the Antichrist; wars have been fueled by religious righteousness that imagines the enemy as dehumanized and in thrall to demonic powers, and so on. To put a human face on spiritual warfare, to ghastly effect, is sadly nothing new.

Conspiracy theories are also nothing new; however, in an age of online algorithmic bundling as discussed above, the human tendency toward taking pleasure in apophenia (the brain's natural tendency to seek for patterns among seemingly disparate things) can be accelerated to new heights precisely on the basis of the platforms and speed of access to information (reliable and otherwise). It is less the content of conspiracies and more the speed and force of their construction that have accelerated in our time.

Theologically, this has at least two detrimental impacts:

1). Fallen Reasoning as Misguided Apophenia: Theology has long spoken of the noetic effects of humanity's fall, that is, the impact of sin upon our very epistemological structures. Sin impacts what we know, how we know it, and the neighbor-love or self-love by which we wield that knowledge.[29] With that in mind, we can speak of a certain mode of apophenic pleasure-seeking in conspiracy thinking that fuels the worst impulses of fallen reason: desire for a kind of gnostic control (i.e., knowing the "real story" over and against official narratives), suspicion bordering on paranoia, and tendencies toward dividing humans into strict categories of good and evil without nuance or complexity. The fallen apophenia of conspiracy thinking, in other words, relates to an economy of epistemological pleasure that is seductive precisely in the way that the fruit of the tree was seductive—you shall become like gods, knowing [who is] good and [who is] evil. It is weaponized Gnosticism whose deleterious effects upon the soul and its capacity to love is, we might say, precisely the opposite of the effects that beauty

---

27. Cf. McGinn, *AntiChrist*.

28. Cf. Richard Beck, *Reviving Old Scratch: Demons and the Devil for Doubters and the Disenchanted* (Minneapolis: Fortress Press, 2016).

29. Cf. Robert Saler, "The Transformation of Reason in Genesis 2–3: Two Options for Theological Interpretation," *Currents in Theology and Mission* 36, no. 4 (2009): 275–87.

mediating the divine ought to have. To the extent that this sort of fallen apophenia is fostered and fed by a theo-aesthetic program, it shrinks the world to literal black and white. If, then, the goal of Death to the World's "black and white" theo-asthetic is to train readers to see color (i.e., plenitude, diversity, fullness of beauty in the church and the world), then this reduction must itself be resisted.

2). Secularized Apocalypse: Death to the World, as we have seen, is premised on the perpetual reminder that "the world" (the saeculum) is transitory and that true reality is "otherworldly." Indeed, its continued rhetorical and aesthetic invocations of otherworldliness are ingredient to its sense of "rebellion against the spirit of the age" precisely to the extent that modernism is premised on forgetfulness or dismissal of another world in favor of pure secularism. However, this makes the tendency of conspiracy theory to take on the form of secularized eschatology (in the form of the immanentization of the evil exercising agency over the events of history) all the more at odds with the core theological insights of Death to the World's vision.

As we have seen, this tension in present in Rose; his writings present a sort of oscillation between otherworldliness and conspiratorial identification of human enemies that is as disorienting as it is seductive. This is, then, one of many places where the Death to the World movement stands at a sort of crossroads, in this case between drawing (in Beck's terms) on the best insights of otherworldliness as an impulse to charity toward fellow humans—demons are demons and humans are not—and, alternatively, allowing the fallen apophenia of conspiracy thinking to allow Rose's legacy to be aesthetically and theologically co-opted into that deadly gnostic economy.[30]

This book is, as stated above, an attempt at a snapshot of a dynamic movement, one still in flux because (I believe) it is still very much alive. The reader who has ventured this far will now perhaps suspect, and rightly so, that my goal (and God willing, the achievement) has been to offer this snapshot as a way of capturing both the flux of the movement's past and present and also the contingency of its future. Will Death to the World continue to harness an energy within global Orthodoxy that is not always fully visible from more mainstream ecclesial/academic vantage points but is nonetheless palpable within much Orthodoxy today? Will the ongoing negotiations between "sustainable" and "sellout," between platform and authenticity, that have always characterized punk and punk-adjacent cultures continue to happen well in the movement? Will the movement be of its time, or be a part of remaking the "spirit of the age," or both? These questions do not admit of fully fleshed out answers, but my contention is that, in the case of Death to the World, the questions are very much worth asking—and that the answers matter to the church and its witness.

---

30. The highly politicized images from Death to the World that we discussed in Chapter 4 (e.g., images of Governor Newsome during the pandemic) would be instances of what I mean by the "aesthetic co-opting" of this side of Rose's legacy.

CONCLUSION

Having reached the end of our discussion of Death to the World, we might ask again: even if we grant that Death to the World is interesting from a historical/cultural perspective, on what basis might we also regard it as theologically interesting?

By this point in the book, the reader might be discerning any number of potential concerns. There are very good reasons why theologians might (and in my view, should) regard much of what has come to be associated with Death to the World as repugnant both theologically and ethically: vaccine denial, dismissal of academic theology, sympathy toward and promulgation of conspiracy theory, and (increasingly) hostility toward regard for the full humanity of those in the LGBTQIA+ community. One can envision a theological treatment of Death to the World in which these deficiencies form the core of the critique and thus the heart of the theological appraisal. Abuse may not obviate right use, as the theological maxim goes, but what if the source is so problematic as to preclude any right use at all? This book has been haunted by this question.

As will be clear to those who have made their way through the preceding chapters, though, I have offered a different take. In order to restate my justification for treating Death to the World's potential as contested rather than straightforwardly malign, I would appeal once again to the history of punk rock. Punk as a sonic culture has, at various points in its history, soundtracked both liberative cultural possibilities and the worst impulses of reactionary counterculture (such as violence and xenophobia as well as anemic corporate commodification). To ask straightforwardly whether punk's existence has been good or bad for humanity is already to distort the answer, because whatever the answer is it cannot be straightforward or simple. So, too, I contend with Death to the World and the theo-aesthetics that it exemplifies.

As indicated throughout the book, from a normative theological perspective, I would suggest that the one contribution that the Death to the World movement makes to theology (both within Eastern Orthodoxy and the broader theological landscape) is to offer an ongoing generative tension between confident apocalypticism keyed to a particular take on a given tradition (Orthodoxy) and the need for Christians to continue to follow Christ in a world of pluralism, ambiguity, and ongoing dynamic interpretation of what it means to love others well. As stated in the Introduction, I do not believe that Death to the World offers any sort of "pure" take on Orthodoxy, mainly because I reject the sort of essentialism that such a judgment would imply. Religious traditions are plural and messy, and this more often than not is a source of vitality and not a problem to be solved.

But that said, "Death to the World helps us appreciate how complicated lived religion is," while true and helpful, is not a robust enough conclusion. Rather, I would like to press things further theologically, and to return to Fr. John Valadez's statement that opens the book. What does it mean for Death to the World to put forth a "black and white" aesthetic—along with a similarly "black and white," that is, uncompromising, theology—in order to train viewers to encounter a church and a world of color?

We saw above that at times Valadez describes this as "bait on a hook"—luring in seekers used to grim aesthetics from punk/metal subcultures so that, once they are in the church, they can experience the full range of the faith (theologically and aesthetically). However, our inquiry has also shown that there are reasons to be cautious about such a simple "bait and switch" understanding of Death to the World's goals for forming the perception of those who engage it. It is true, as I have stressed throughout the book, that Death to the World's clear emphasis, from the time of Marler forward, is replacement of one subculture (punk/metal) with another (Orthodoxy). However, such a straightforward replacement has not, as we have seen, been the legacy of Death to the World; rather, the movement has had a shaping influence upon much of Orthodoxy in the United States in particular.

This point about the shaping influence of Death to the World is a crucial one. On an authorial note, the center at the seminary where I teach has often been approached by Eastern Orthodox jurisdictions to help conduct surveys related to Orthodox life in the United States (evaluation being one of the center's specialties), and from that data it is clear that many priests in the United States are aware that for catechumens and inquirers especially, online Orthodoxy plays a major role both in cultivating their interest in the faith and in their understanding of faith's content. To the extent that Death to the World is an influential aesthetic and theological source within online Orthodoxy, it is certainly safe to conclude that, as Death to the World goes, so goes much of thinking of those attracted to Orthodoxy in this country. Thus, the movement's theological direction matters for the church.

Quo Vadis?

Throughout this book, I have attempted to build a case that Death to the World exists at a crossroads. For reasons that, as I have argued, are endemic to both punk as a cultural form and apocalyptic as a theological category, the theo-aesthetics of rebellion lend themselves to a perpetual critique of the "principalities and powers" (Eph. 6:12) of this world.

Even former enthusiasts who have since cooled on Death to the World attest to its ongoing influence in their faith, even as they acknowledge a number of ambiguities. An Orthodox librarian named Ryan Timothy Laferney recounts,

I came into the Orthodox Church—looking for the true, authentic, early Church. I found it in Eastern Orthodoxy. I grew up a non-believing, militant atheist and was a participant in the Midwest punk and hardcore scenes, and eventually got into metal and its subgenres (although now I am mainly interested in folk and country music). So, the aesthetics of Death to the World really appealed to me in my early twenties, and of course, Fr. Seraphim Rose was an attractive figure to me, as someone who felt disenfranchised. I converted en masse with a group of maybe 20 other early twenty somethings who were punks, metalheads, tattooed rejects, etc. that were seeking the truth. Death to the World even helped my parents understand my newfound faith. The aesthetics were something they were used to seeing me engage with. I found Death to the World after already being familiar with Orthodoxy and on my road to being received into the church. The bookstore, Desert Wisdom Books, at the old St. Mary of Egypt Orthodox Church location on 31st and Troost in Kansas City, MO. had copies of some of the zines produced in the '90s. I purchased a chunk of them and read them dutifully. I had experienced despair, and depression, and the stories I was reading from others and the stories of saints and martyrs resonated with me. I think Death to the World helped me realize there was a place for me in the church. As I have grown older, I have become less enchanted with Death to the World, especially now that it has an on-line platform. There have been some posts from their social media presence that have given me pause. And I wrestle with Death to the World as a commodity. But I also wonder if my personal aesthetic tastes have changed. I am certainly enamored with Orthodox worship and the beauty of the faith. But I am no longer really drawn to extreme aesthetics and ideas. I feel like I have mellowed out. Perhaps that is intentional on part of founders of the zine? However, I will say, that I believe Death to the World has helped lead many folks to the true faith and I think God has used it for some good.[1]

Matt Stein, who as mentioned above was at St. Platina during the formation of the original zine, reflects poignantly on a similar transition in his own regard for the zine and the movement.

For me, Death to the World was an organic, living movement connected as much to a time and a place as to a philosophy and worldview. In one sense it was born into existence, lived a life, and after a time reposed.

Not only was it a philosophy and worldview it was a working hypothesis proposing that elements of truth seeking were embedded, even if misdirected, within punk rock and adjacent youth subcultures.

For many, myself included, this hypothesis proved true. The same energy that electrified me when I was first exposed to punk rock at twelve years of age was again present when I was first exposed to and heard about the ideas at the roots of Death to the World at twenty-one years of age.

1. Private communication with author, October 4, 2022.

... Justin [Marler's] vision of punks to monks baptized and resurrected my old relationship and respect for punk. His vision, which was foundational to Death to the World, helped make accessible an ancient and transformative expression of Christianity to my modern, aimless soul. Had the connection between punk and monastic subcultures not been recognized and articulated by Justin, I might have never been able to sustain living at the monastery. I often struggled, hanging on by a thread, especially for the first few weeks of living in a monastic setting. Justin, his vision, and Theophany Skete all helped keep this thread from breaking and afforded me enough time for this ancient Christian way of life to sprout and take root in my body, mind, and soul ...

Death to the World was but one part of an intense group of truth seeking youth who had come of age and were involved in the underground punk/hardcore/metal/alternative subcultures of the mid 80's to early 90's. There was absolutely nothing like it. This little spark of a movement, both unique and powerful, merged together the most unlikely of subcultures, punks and monks. It not only gave deep meaning to lost souls, it literally saved lives.[2]

Stein goes on to reflect,

In retrospect, from the perspective of one who was there but was also an outsider (I was not part of DTTW's creation and left the monastery just as it was beginning to grow), I think of the movement largely as a bridge (for some) into Orthodoxy. Yet, Orthodoxy in the modern world, especially in America, is so divided and multifaceted. Orthodoxy is not a monolith and there are many different legitimate approach's [sic] and perspectives, none of which are perfect. After years of being tossed about by claims that this or that perspective was the truest Orthodox way, I now consider these different perspectives and approaches as counterweights helping to keep everyone honest and nearer to a golden mean. Movements like Death to the World are best when they take one to the narthex of the Church and don't attempt to go much further than this. It's better as a bridge than as a spiritual guide that risks inadvertently thrusting individuals into the chaotic maze of factions, politics, opinions, personalities, and prejudices that can suck the soul out one's spiritual life. All that enter the Church will be forced, to some degree, to navigate these realities. Movements like Death to the World should avoid taking up the mantle of any of these various internecine struggles. Political pundits and personality cults are all too willing to exploit the youthful idealism, energy, and the need for purpose and mentorship of young converts. We should avoid, as much as possible, more spiritual lives being sacrificed to the factionalism that thrives in the chaotic overlapping jurisdictions of the American Orthodox landscape.[3]

---

2. Matt Stein, "Apocalypse of Youth," *These Buried Sparks*, accessed October 9, 2022, https://theseburiedsparks.substack.com/p/apocalypse-of-youth.

3. Ibid.

What Stein is articulating here, again, is not radically different from Valadez's notion of "bait on a hook;" however, in accord with what I have been suggesting throughout the book, the bait itself is not neutral and the results of the "hook" are neither unidirectional nor inevitable. Spiritual vigilance is required on the part of those producing this content as well as those consuming and promulgating it.

The previous chapter of this book was my attempt to outline in more specific fashion what this vigilance might entail, and at what crossroads the Death to the World movement stands. It seems important to reiterate at the end of the book, as I stated in the beginning, that I write as a fan of the movement and with critical appreciation for its achievements (as well as hope in its potential). But I also write as a theologian afraid of the gathering forces that have shown signs of being able to successfully co-opt the movement by capitalizing on some core tensions within Rose, within punk, and within apocalyptic as a whole. Both my fandom and my fear are real.

Stein concludes:

> The first generation Death to the World produced fruits, the seeds from which sprouted into a second generation. I know little of this new iteration. I was no longer a youth when it came into being. It's [sic] existence mainly caused me to reflect on my experiences around the original Death to the World. To be honest, I tried to put that part of my Orthodox experience behind me. But, for better or worse, it's a foundational and inseparable part of both my adult life and my Orthodox life. I appreciate it immensely. My hope is that the second generation Death to the World learns from the experiences, both good and bad, of the first generation. Death to the World must be ever vigilant not to provide cannon fodder for these self-serving and soul crushing wars within Orthodoxy. It should always strive to stay true to and focused on its original spirit and vision.[4]

Throughout this book, particularly in the earlier chapters, I have endeavored to articulate what Stein (and I) believes to be the main features of this "original spirit and vision:" deep resonance with the struggles of youth who see the degeneracy of the economic, political, and religious systems whose brokenness holds the world in thrall; a hagiographical collapsing of the distance between the courageous lives of the saints and our own lives; and a sense of deep purpose in the face of the threat of nihilism as manifested both philosophically and culturally. That said, it is clear from Stein's text that he writes from a position of awareness as to what the fruits of Orthodox "factionalism" look like when movements such as Death to the World "take up the mantle" of both religious division and attendant culture wars. His wisdom is salutary.

Late in life, Fr. Seraphim Rose himself seems to have recognized some of these same ambiguities, including in relation to the convert and anti-nihilistic fervor.

---

4. Ibid.

His biographer, Hieromonk Damascene, points out that Rose saw troubling signs of "hyper-correctness" about Orthodoxy and a zealotry that lacked love emerging within converts especially as witnessed in the following excerpt:

> During the last decade of his life, Fr. Seraphim poured an incredible amount of time and energy into the question of "super-correctness," having to uphold the Orthodox consciousness handed down from his Fathers against the many idiosyncrasies of the neo-traditionalist "theology." Not only were articles needed, but also carefully thought-out answers to the many who came to him wondering about the new tone that was being set in the Church.
>
> ... we should consider the effect that this matter had in rounding out Fr. Seraphim's message to the modern world. As we have seen, super-correctness (and not always in the obvious forms mentioned above) is a big temptation for Orthodox people of these latter times, when "the love of many grows cold." Indeed, correctness is built into the very word "Orthodox," which means "right worship." A key question for our days, which Fr. Seraphim had to face, was: How does one remain a right (Orthodox) believer without becoming self-righteous?
>
> It was because Fr. Seraphim had a head-on collision with "correct" extremism that he was able to help his contemporaries out of this ditch. If he had not had it, it is likely that his writings would have proved one-sided. Even if he had avoided this pitfall himself, his words would not have been able to prevent less balanced individuals from going off the deep end on the right side. As it stands now, however, his message to people of today is full of sobering warnings against renovationism on the right as well as on the left, against legalism and loveless externalism under the guise of "traditionalism" ...
>
> [Rose] himself had been a convert to "zealot Orthodoxy"; and it was necessary that he go deeper into the phenomenon of zealotry, which by itself was not the answer. By dealing with it, and even more by suffering over it throughout many years, he had been forced to eradicate vestiges of cold elitism from his Christian faith, even while maintaining his devotion to the cause of "true Orthodoxy."[5]

One way of thinking about some of the more troubling aspects of the Death to the World movement that we have been considering in this book is to see them precisely as "less balanced individuals going off the deep end," even as I have also endeavored to demonstrate why I think that there are significant technological and ideological forces at work that encourage precisely such lack of balance (and thus warn us against ascribing the main problems to "individuals"). To be sure, the battles against "super-correctness" that Rose anticipated and fought were not exactly the same as the concerning trends that we have outlined in this book, and it is problematic to assume with too much certainty how Rose might have regarded a number of contemporary currents in Orthodox thinking that cite him as a key

---

5. Damascene, *Father Seraphim Rose*, 531–2.

influence. However, the spirit of Rose's correction as well as his goals here is very much in line with what I am advocating. Put directly, to the extent that the Death to the World movement regards Rose as a (literal) patron saint of the movement and what it is trying to achieve in Orthodoxy as well as in broader American culture, then his humility and vigilance against excess should receive the same emulation as his rebellion against the "spirit of the modern age."

What would this mean?

Because much of this book has been devoted to demonstrating that, in the case of Death to the World as in so much of life, the lines between what is theological and what is political are blurry and sometimes inextricable, it would be naïve and unrealistic to frame the choice as one between a movement that avoids politics entirely and one that engages it without reservation. Orthodoxy in the United States and globally seems destined to have to navigate thorny issues of power, authority, and geopolitics until the end. And neither art nor theology that has a word for life under the principalities and powers can be relevant or resonant; theo-aesthetic formation requires truth-telling in all its facets.

But we can, in the end, envision a theological rebellion of a different sort, of the sort that Rose in his better moments saw and to which Death to the World at its best points. One in which, being grounded precisely in the witness of the saints and the sort of uncompromising devotion to God that Death to the World has advocated unwaveringly since its inception, we refuse co-optation into the most reductive and conspiratorial politics and culture wars of the day in order to present a face of peace, openness, and humility to a broken yet beautifully diverse world. This is, to be clear, its own sort of political as well as spiritual stance. We can be formed by the stark punk blast of Death to the World in order to stir up this rebellion against all that would teach us to reason according to the standard divisions and polarities of "the world's logic," and speak in ways that are truly useless—"as dead"—to the arguments that dominate headlines and the blogosphere alike. And this not so we are indifferent to our neighbors who suffer under the world's brokenness, but precisely so we can engage that brokenness on heaven's own terms. We are then in a position, as Valadez states, to encounter the full beauty of the church, not as a vehicle to put the world to death, but to see the life of God that pervades the world that God created, loves, and redeems in beauty and truth.

BIBLIOGRAPHY

A Devotional Heart. "Father John Valadez on 'Death to the World.' Fr. Seraphim Rose, Fr. Nektarios, and Fr. Turbo." Accessed May 27, 2023. https://www.youtube.com/watch?v=v9XeeHIcBjk&t=2013s.

Abraham, Ibrahim (ed.). *Christian Punk: Identity and Performance*. London: Bloomsbury, 2020.

Anatolios, Khaled. *Deification through the Cross: An Eastern Christian Theology of Salvation*. Grand Rapids, MI: Eerdmans, 2020.

Athitakis, Mark. "A Punk's Progress." *San Francisco Weekly*, July 12, 2000. https://www.sfweekly.com/music/riff-raff-146/.

Audette-Longo, Michael. "'Feel the Noise:' The Promotional Allure of Punk Fanzines." In *Punk, Fanzines, and DIY Cultures in a Global World: Fast, Furious, and Xerox*. Edited by Paula Guerra and Pedro Quintela. London: Palgrave MacMillan, 2020.

Bailey, Father Spyridon. *Orthodoxy and the Kingdom of Satan*. Self-published, FeedaReed.com, 2017.

Baker, Kimberly. "Augustine's Doctrine of the Totus Christus: Reflecting on the Church as Sacrament of Unity." *Horizons: The Journal of the College Theological Society* 37, no. 1 (Spring, 2010): 7–24.

Beck, Richard. *Reviving Old Scratch: Demons and the Devil for Doubters and the Disenchanted*. Minneapolis: Fortress Press, 2016.

Benjamin, Walter. *The Work of Art in the Age of Mechanical Reproduction*. Translated by J. A. Underwood. Harlow: Penguin Books, 2008.

Boone, David. "Punkocalypse: Case Study of an Apocalyptic Youth Movement in Modern Times." Unpublished article. Accessed May 27, 2023. https://www.academia.edu/19489349/Punkocalypse_Case_Study_of_an_Apocalyptic_Youth_Movement_in_Modern_Times.

Bourdieu, Pierre. *The Field of Cultural Production*. Translated by Randal Johnson. New York: Columbia University Press, 1993.

Bouteneff, Peter, Jeffers Engelhardt, and Robert Saler (eds.). *Arvo Pärt: Sounding the Sacred*. New York: Fordham, 2020.

Brewin, Kester. *Mutiny! Why We Love Pirates and How They Can Save Us*. London: Vaux, 2016.

Brown, Emily. "Death to the World: The Last True Rebellion." *The Outline*, December 21, 2016. https://theoutline.com/post/715/death-to-the-world.

Burgess, John P. *Holy Rus': The Rebirth of Orthodoxy in the New Russia*. Oxford: Oxford University Press, 2017.

Butler, Anthea. *White Evangelical Racism: The Politics of Morality in America*. Chapel Hill, NC: UNC Press, 2021.

Campbell, Heidi A. *Digital Creatives and the Rethinking of Religious Authority*. New York: Routledge, 2020.

Carrette, Jeremy R. and Richard King. *Selling Spirituality: The Silent Takeover of Religion*. London: Routledge, 2004.

Collins, John (ed.). *Apocalypse: The Morphology of a Genre*. Missoula, MT: Scholars Press, 1979.
Collins, John (ed.). "Apocalyptic Eschatology in the Ancient World." In *The Oxford Handbook of Eschatology*. Edited by Jerry L. Walls. Oxford: Oxford University Press, 2008.
Cone, James. *God of the Oppressed*. Maryknoll, NY: Orbis, 1997.
Congdon, David W. "Eschatologizing Apocalyptic: An Assessment of the Present Conversation on Pauline Apocalyptic." In *Apocalyptic and the Future of Theology: With and beyond Louis J. Martyn*. Edited by Joshua B. Davis and Douglas Harink. Eugene, OR: Cascade, 2012.
Crissman, Marina and John Valdez. "Death to the World: An Orthodox Punk Zine Revived and Revisited." Interviewed by Geraldine Fagan and RTE. *Road to Emmaus: A Journal of Orthodox Faith and Culture* 47 (January 17, 2018): 28–9. https://static1.squarespace.com/static/5e78f10494c7b26bc99e2fd2/t/5e8e23c472407957667f3e67/1586373572976/47.DEATH_TO_THE_WORLD.pdf.
Damascene, Hieromonk. *Father Seraphim Rose: His Life and Works*. Platina, CA: St. Herman of Alaska Press, 2003.
Davis, G. M. *Antichrist: The Fulfillment of Globalization*. Jordanville, NY: Uncut Mountain Press, 2022.
Death to the World. "2020 Vision: From Blindness to Sight in the Age of Collapse." *Death to the World*, no. 27 (January 8, 2021). https://deathtotheworld.com/articles/2020-vision-from-blindness-to-sight-in-the-age-of-collapse/.
Death to the World. "A Lot of Speculation." Facebook, April 30, 2020. https://www.facebook.com/DTTWzine/posts/pfbid02tr3HGbQW4HaRKa8cZVRAQFjxFA52ECjEnVq36R7UZGdaa1hmpwQbVhB4dK5FzZZTl.
Death to the World. "About: What Do We Mean by Death to the World?" Last modified April 3, 2020. https://deathtotheworld.com/about/.
Death to the World. "Saint Febronia: Beauty Bathed in Blood." *Death to the World* (July 10, 2014). https://deathtotheworld.com/articles/saint-febronia-beauty-bathed-in-blood/.
Death to the World. "Two Deaths." *Death to the World* (March 11, 2013). https://deathtotheworld.com/articles/two-deaths/.
de Certeau, Michel. *The Practice of Everyday Life*. 3rd ed. Translated by Steven Rendall. Berkeley: University of California Press, 2011.
Denysenko, Nicholas. *The Church's Unholy War: Russia's Invasion of Ukraine and Orthodoxy*. Eugene, OR: Cascade, 2023.
Denysenko, Nicholas. *The Orthodox Church in Ukraine: A Century of Separation*. Ithaca, NY: Cornell University Press, 2018.
Dilva, Guillermo Andres Duque and Cristina Del Prado Higuera. "Political Theology and Covid-19: Agamben's Critique of Science as a New 'Pandemic Religion.'" *Open Theology* 7, no. 1 (October 5, 2021).
Duncombe, Stephen. *Notes from Underground: Zines and the Politics of Alternative Culture*. 3rd ed. Portland: Microcosm Publishing, 2017.
Duncombe, Stephen and Maxwell Tremblay. *White Riot: Punk Rock and the Politics of Race*. London: Verso, 2011.
Elliott, Neil. *The Arrogance of Nations: Reading Romans in the Shadow of Empire*. Minneapolis: Fortress, 2008.
Engelhart, Jeffers. "Arvo Pärt and the Idea of a Christian Europe: The Musical Effects and Affects of Post-Ideological Religion." In *Resounding Transcendence: Transitions*

in Music, Religion, and Ritual. Edited by Jeffers Engelhardt and Philip V. Bohlman. Oxford: Oxford University Press, 2016: 214–32.

Ensminger, David A. *Visual Vitriol: The Street Art and Subcultures of the Punk and Hardcore Generations.* Jackson: University Press of Mississippi, 2011.

Fisher, Mark. *Capitalist Realism: Is There No Alternative?* London: Zero Books, 2009.

Floridoxy. "Father John Valadez and Death to the World." Accessed May 27, 2023. https://www.youtube.com/watch?v=RwQIidC1US4.

Forde, Gerhard O. *Justification by Faith: A Matter of Death and Life.* Eugene, OR: Wipf and Stock, 2012.

Granholm, Kennet. "Metal, the End of the World, and Radical Environmentalism: Ecological Apocalypse in the Lyrics of Earth Crisis." In *Anthems of Apocalypse: Popular Music and Apocalyptic Thought.* Edited by Christopher Partridge. Sheffield: Phoenix Press, 2012: 27–42.

Griffith, R. Marie. *Moral Combat: How Sex Divided American Christians and Fractured American Politics.* New York: Basic, 2017.

Griffiths, Paul. *Decreation: The Last Things of All Creatures.* Waco, TX: Baylor, 2014.

Groppe, Elizabeth T. (ed.). *Seeing with the Eyes of the Heart: Cultivating a Sacramental Imagination in an Age of Pornography.* Washington, DC: Catholic University of America Press, 2020.

Haenfler, Ross. *Straight Edge: Hardcore Punk, Clean Living Youth, and Social Change.* New York: Rutgers, 2006.

Hart, David Bentley. "Orthodoxy in America and America's Orthodoxies." Lecture given at Fordham University, New York, NY, October 2, 2017. https://www.youtube.com/watch?v=WU3y_h47ByE.

Hart, David Bentley. *Tradition and Apocalypse: An Essay on the Future of Christian Belief.* Ada, MI: Baker, 2022.

Hebdige, Dick. *Subculture: The Meaning of Style.* London: Routledge, 1988.

Herbel, D. Oliver. *Turning to Tradition: Converts and the Making of an American Orthodox Church.* Oxford: Oxford University Press, 2013.

Hollinger, David. *After Tongues of Cloven Fire: Protestant Liberalism in Modern American History.* Princeton, NJ: Princeton University Press, 2013.

Hopko, Thomas. "The Sunday of Orthodoxy." February 19, 2010. In *Speaking the Truth in Love*, podcast. https://www.ancientfaith.com/podcasts/hopko/the_sunday_of_orthodoxy.

Howard, Jay R. and John R. Streck. *Apostles of Rock: The Splintered World of Contemporary Christian Music.* Lexington, MA: University Press of Kentucky, 2004.

Jain, Andrea. *Selling Yoga: From Counterculture to Pop Culture.* Oxford: Oxford University Press, 2014.

Jennings Jr., Theodore W. *Outlaw Justice: The Messianic Politics of Paul.* Palo Alto, CA: Stanford, 2013.

Jennings Jr., Theodore W. *Reading Derrida/Thinking Paul: On Justice.* Palo Alto, CA: Stanford, 2005.

Joas, Hans. *Faith as an Option: Possible Futures for Christianity.* Palo Alto, CA: Stanford, 2014.

Johnson, Buck. "It Takes Humility to Understand What's Happening," with Father Turbo Qualls, July 13, 2022. In *Counterflow*, podcast. https://deathtotyrants.libsyn.com/ep-217-it-takes-humility-to-understand-whats-happening-with-father-turbo-qualls.

Käsemann, Ernst. "The Beginnings of Christian Theology." In *New Testament Questions of Today.* Translated by William John Montague. London: SCM, 1969.

Kuhn, Gabriel. *Sober Living for the Revolution Hardcore Punk, Straight Edge, and Radical Politics*. Oakland, CA: PM Press, 2010.
Lincoln, Bruce. *Authority: Construction and Corrosion*. Chicago: University of Chicago Press, 1995.
Lofton, Kathryn. *Consuming Religion*. Chicago: University of Chicago Press, 2017.
Lynch, Zechariah. "Sinister Psychosis and the Remembrance of God." Accessed May 29, 2023. https://deathtotheworld.com/articles/sinister-psychosis-and-the-remembrance-of-god/.
Lynch, Zechariah. "The Cosmic Significance of Tsar Nicholas II." *Death to the World*. July 17, 2020. https://deathtotheworld.com/articles/the-cosmic-significance-of-tsar-nicholas-ii/.
Marler, Justin. Introduction to *Death to the World* 1 (1994). https://deathtotheworld.com/articles/death-to-the-world-issue-1/.
Marler, Justin. "Justin Marler: From Metal to the Monastery." Interviewed by Brother Augustine. May 27, 2022. https://www.youtube.com/watch?v=Ijc8DWem__Q.
Marler, Justin. "Justin Marler of 'The Quick and the Dead.'" Interviewed by Simon Head. November 30, 2015. In *Apologue*. http://apologue.ca/epi-57-justin-marler-of-quick-and-the-dead/.
Marler, Justin. "Justin Marler: Warring against Yourself." Interviewed by Shiloh Coleman. November 14, 2018. https://www.shilohcoleman.com/blog/2018-justinmarler.
Marler, Justin. "The Failure of Hedonism." *Death to the World* 27. Accessed May 29, 2023. https://deathtotheworld.com/articles/the-failure-of-hedonism/.
Marler, Justin. "The Last True Rebellion with Justin Marler." Interviewed by Buck Johnson. June 14, 2022. https://www.youtube.com/watch?v=7AkELO2V8kM.
Marler, Justin. "Youth of the Apocalypse with Justin Marler." Interviewed by the Mad Ones. July 6, 2022. https://www.youtube.com/watch?v=OhGWSn2fA9E&t=5296s.
Marler, Justin and Andrew Wermuth. *Youth of the Apocalypse and the Last True Rebellion*. Spruce Island, AK: St. Herman of Alaska, 1995.
Martin, John Jeffries. *A Beautiful Ending: The Apocalyptic Imagination and the Making of the Modern World*. New Haven, CT: Yale, 2022.
Mathewes-Green, Frederica. *At the Corner of East and Now: A Modern Life in Ancient Christian Orthodoxy*. Chesterton, IN: Ancient Faith Publishing, 1999.
Mattson, Kevin. *We're Not Here to Entertain: Punk Rock, Ronald Reagan, and the Real Culture War of 1980's America*. Oxford: Oxford University Press, 2020.
McGinn, Bernard. *AntiChrist: Two Thousand Years of the Human Fascination with Evil*. New York: Columbia University Press, 2000.
McInroy, Mark. "Spiritual Perception and Beauty: On Looking and Letting Appear." In *Perceiving Things Divine: Towards a Constructive Account of Spiritual Perception*. Edited by Frederick D. Aquino and Paul Gavrilyuk. Oxford: Oxford University Press, 2022.
Michelson, Patrick. *Beyond the Monastery Walls: The Ascetic Revolution in Russian Orthodox Thought, 1814–1914*. Madison, WI: The University of Wisconsin Press, 2017.
Moberg, Marcus. *Christian Metal: History, Ideology, Scene*. London: Bloomsbury, 2015.
Muggleton, David. *Inside Subculture: The Postmodern Meaning of Style*. Oxford: Berg, 2002.
Mullen, Lincoln A. *The Chance of Salvation: A History of Conversion in America*. Cambridge, MA: Harvard, 2017.
Nietzsche, Friedrick. *The Gay Science*. Translated by Walter Kaufmann. New York: Vintage, 1974.

O'Regan, Cyril. *Theology and the Spaces of Apocalyptic*. Milwaukee: Marquette University Press, 2009.

Pagels, Elaine. *Adam, Eve, and the Serpent*. New York: Penguin, 1988.

Papanikolaou, Aristotle and Elizabeth Prodromou (eds.). *Thinking through Faith: New Perspectives from Orthodox Christian Scholars*. Yonkers, NY: St. Vladimir's Seminary Press, 2008.

Partridge, Christopher (ed.). *Anthems of Apocalypse: Popular Music and Apocalyptic Thought*. Sheffield: Phoenix Press, 2012.

Parvu, Iustin. "Enter." In *Viata Parintelui Iustin Pirvu*. Translated by John Sanidopoulos. Reprinted in *Death to the World* 28 (January 29, 2023). https://deathtotheworld.com/articles/enter/.

Patitsas, Timothy George. *The Ethics of Beauty*. Boston: St. Nicholas Press, 2022.

Patton, Raymond. *Punk Crisis: The Global Punk Rock Revolution*. Oxford: Oxford University Press, 2018.

Peck, John. "Full Impact Faith: An Interview with Fr. Turbo Qualls." Accessed May 27, 2023. https://journeytoorthodoxy.com/2017/07/full-impact-faith-an-interview-with-fr-turbo-qualls/.

Perry, Samuel L. *The Flag and the Cross: White Christian Nationalism and the Threat to American Democracy*. Oxford: Oxford University Press, 2022.

Ray, Darby Kathleen. *Deceiving the Devil: Atonement, Abuse, and Ransom*. Cleveland, OH: The Pilgrim Press, 1988.

Reagan, Micheal. "In Spirit and Truth." *Death to the World* 13 (February 2, 2013). https://deathtotheworld.com/articles/zine-articles/in-spirit-and-truth-issue-13/.

Riccardi-Swartz, Sarah. *Between Heaven and Russia: Religious Conversion and Political Apostasy in Appalachia*. New York: Fordham, 2022.

Riccardi-Swartz, Sarah. "Holy Pixels: The Transformation of Eastern Orthodox Icons." In *Digital Orthodoxy in the Post-Soviet World*. Edited by Mikhail Suslov. Stuttgart: Ibidem-Verlag, 2016.

Rosa, Hartmut. *Social Acceleration: A New Theory of Modernity*. Translated by Jonathan Trejo-Mathys. New York: Columbia Press, 2015.

Rose, Seraphim. *God's Revelation to the Human Heart*. 5th ed. Platina, CA: St. Herman of Alaska Monastery, 2007.

Rose, Seraphim. "Living the Orthodox Worldview." Transcript in the *Orthodox Word* 18, no. 4 (105) (July-August 1982): 160–76. https://classicalchristianity.com/2011/11/19/fr-seraphim-roses-orthodox-world-view/.

Rose, Seraphim. *Nihilism: The Root of the Revolution of the Modern Age*. Reprint ed. Platina, CA: St. Herman of Alaska Press, 2001.

Rose, Seraphim. *Orthodoxy and the Religion of the Future*. Platina, CA: St. Herman of Alaska Brotherhood Press, 1975.

Rose, Seraphim. "The Orthodox Survival Course." Unpublished work. Accessed May 29, 2023. https://www.patristicfaith.com/orthodox-christianity/the-orthodox-survival-course-by-father-seraphim-rose/.

Rossing, Barbara. *The Rapture Exposed: The Message of Hope in the Book of Revelation*. New York: Basic Books, 2005.

Saler, Robert. *All These Things into Position: What Theology Can Learn from Radiohead*. Eugene, OR: Cascade, 2019.

Saler, Robert. *Between Magisterium and Marketplace*. Minneapolis, MN: Fortress Press, 2014.

Saler, Robert. "The Transformation of Reason in Genesis 2–3: Two Options for Theological Interpretation." *Currents in Theology and Mission* 36, no. 4 (2009).

Saler, Robert. *Theologia Crucis*. Eugene, OR: Cascade, 2016.
Saler, Robert and Kevin Clay. "Christian Grimm of 13th Vigil on Art of the Apocalypse." Accessed May 27, 2023, https://www.youtube.com/watch?v=b_Fq1g2wWT8&t=8s.
Sanchez, Gabriel. "Death to Death to the World." *Opus Publicum*, December 30, 2016. http://opuspublicum.com/death-to-death-to-the-world/.
Scupoli, Lorenzo. *Unseen Warfare: The Spiritual Combat and Path to Paradise of Lorenzo Scupoli*. Edited by Theophan the Recluse and Nicodemus of the Holy Mountain. New York: St. Vladimir's Seminary Press, 2007.
Siguenza, Carmen and Esther Robello. "Byun-Chul Han: Covid-19 Has Reduced Us to a 'Society of Survival.'" *Eruactiv*, May 24, 2020. https://www.euractiv.com/section/global-europe/interview/byung-chul-han-covid-19-has-reduced-us-to-a-society-of-survival/.
Slagle, Amy. *The Eastern Orthodox Church in the Spiritual Marketplace: American Conversions to Orthodox Christianity*. DeKalb, IL: Northern Illinois University Press, 2011.
Sleep. "Stillborn." Track 1 on *Volume 1*. Very Small Records, 1991.
Smith, Justin E. H. *The Internet Is Not What You Think It Is: A History, a Philosophy, a Warning*. Princeton, NJ: Princeton University Press, 2022.
St. John of Damascus. *On Holy Images*. Translated by Mary H. Allies. London: Baker, 1898.
Stein, Matt. "Apocalypse of Youth." *These Buried Sparks*. Accessed October 9, 2022. https://theseburiedsparks.substack.com/p/apocalypse-of-youth.
Stein, Matt. "Worlds Colliding." *These Buried Sparks*, January 22, 2022. https://theseburiedsparks.substack.com/p/worlds-colliding.
Stievermann, Jan, Philip Goff, and Detlef Junker. "General Introduction." *Religion and the Marketplace in the United States*. Edited by Stievermann, Goff, and Junker. Oxford: Oxford University Press, 2015.
Stewart, Francis. *Punk Rock Is My Religion: Straight Edge Punk and "Religious" Identity*. New York: Routledge, 2017.
Stith, Deborah Sengupta. "The Unbroken Circle." December 4, 2015. http://specials.mystatesman.com/austin-punk-monk/.
Sunkara, Bhaskar. *The Socialist Manifesto: The Case for Radical Politics in an Era of Extreme Inequality*. New York: Basic Books, 2019.
Sutton, Matthew Avery. *American Apocalypse: A History of Modern Evangelicalism*. Cambridge, MA: Harvard, 2017.
Taylor, Mark Lewis. *The Executed God: The Way of the Cross in Lockdown America*. 2nd ed. Minneapolis, MN: Fortress Press, 2015.
The Orthodox Logos. "Interview with Christian Grimm of 13th Vigil." Accessed May 28, 2023. https://www.youtube.com/watch?v=4X-urb9PSh0.
Thompson, Stacy. *Punk Productions: Unfinished Business*. Albany: SUNY Press, 2004.
Toop, David. *Ocean of Sound: Aether Talk, Ambient Sound, and Imaginary Worlds*. New York: Serpents Tail Press, 2001.
Tsakiridou, Cornelia A. *Icons in Time, Persons in Eternity: Orthodox Theology and the Aesthetics of the Christian Image*. London: Routledge, 2013.
Uscinski, Joseph E. and Joseph Parent. *American Conspiracy Theories*. Oxford: Oxford University Press, 2014.
Valadez, John. "Arriving at the Last True Rebellion." Accessed August 14, 2022. https://deathtotheworld.com/articles/arriving-at-the-last-true-rebellion/.
Valadez, John. "Catechetical School." *St. Timothy Orthodox Church*. Accessed May 27, 2023. http://www.sttimothy.net/index.php/category/recordings/.

Valadez, John. "Other Resources." *St. Timothy Orthodox Church*, May 4, 2019. http://www.sttimothy.net/index.php/2019/05/04/other-resources/.

Valadez, John. "The Orthodox World View: Spiritual Formation and Discernment Today." *St. Thomas Orthodox Church*, August 13, 2020. http://www.sttimothy.net/index.php/2020/08/13/survival-course-for-orthodox-christians/.

Ward, Benedicta (trans.). *The Sayings of the Desert Fathers, the Alphabetical Collection*. Kalamazoo, MI: Cistercian Publications, 1984.

Westphal, Merold. *Suspicion and Faith: The Religious Uses of Modern Atheism*. New York: Fordham University Press, 1993.

Whitehead, Andrew L. and Samuel L. Perry. *Taking America Back for God: Christian Nationalism in the United States*. Oxford: Oxford University Press, 2022.

Whitelock, Edward and David Janssen. *Apocalypse Jukebox: The End of the World in American Popular Music*. Berkeley: Soft Skull, 2009.

Wu, Timothy. *The Attention Merchants: The Epic Scramble to Get inside Our Heads*. New York: Knopf, 2016.

Wuthnow, Robert. *The Restructuring of American Religion: Society and Faith since World War II*. Princeton, NJ: Princeton University Press, 1988.

INDEX

academic theology 12, 49, 74, 101, 113
acts-based Christianity 62
aesthetic objects 2 n.3
aesthetics 11, 17, 20–2, 28, 31–2, 34, 42–4, 51, 58 n.26, 69, 73, 76, 94, 97, 101–2, 104, 106, 108–9, 115
Agamben, Giorgio 87
algorithmic clustering 67
Allin, G. G. 54
ambiguity 51, 108, 113–14, 117
American Orthodoxy. *See* Eastern Orthodox Christianity
American Russophile 84
anarcho-punk 12, 96
Ancient Faith Radio 71
"Anti Anti Christ Gun Club" 75
Antichrist 21, 35–6, 47, 72, 74, 81–2, 84–5, 86–7 n.18, 88, 93, 103, 110–11. *See also* Christian/Christianity
anti-ecumenism 37 n.22. *See also* ecumenism
anti-essentialism 14. *See also* essentialism
anti-Marxism 85. *See also* Marxism/Marxist
antimodernism/antimodernist 4, 16, 55. *See also* modernity/modernism
Antiochian Orthodox Church 1, 7 n.10, 9, 17, 71, 79–80
apocalypse/apocalyptic/apocalypticism 22, 35–6, 47–55, 50 n.16, 57, 60, 68, 72, 74–5, 81, 83–4, 92–3, 95–7, 99–100, 109, 111, 117
  apocalyptic declension 34, 88, 92, 95
  apocalyptic literature 48 n.10, 49
  secularized 112
  zine to movement 51–5
apophenia/apophenic 111–12
Apostolic Church 108 n.24
Aquinas, Thomas 35 n.18
ascetic/asceticism 1–2, 5, 7, 10 n.12, 19, 21, 30–1, 39–40, 43, 46–7, 63,

atheism/atheist 38, 115
Augustine 33, 47
authentic/authenticity 27, 30, 39, 42, 50, 54, 62, 69, 106, 112, 115
authority 22, 66, 76–7, 82–3, 88, 92, 96–7, 119
  in US Orthodoxy 77–81
autocephaly/autocephalous church 79–80

Bailey, Bonnie 43 n.5
Balthasar, Hans Urs von 2, 3 n.4
baptism 9, 97, 99, 104
St. Barnabas (Antiochian) in Costa Mesa, CA 66
beauty 2, 22, 46, 73, 107, 111–12, 115, 119
  Tsakiridou on 2 n.3
Beck, Richard 111–12
"Begone Fordhamite" 74
Benjamin, Walter 107
Bible study 62–3, 65
Black Flag band 28
Black liberation theology 100 n.12
black magic 87 n.18
Bolsheviks/Bolshevism 81–5, 88–9
Book of Acts 31
Book of Revelations 86–7 n.18
bookstores 32–3, 56, 65, 74–5, 115. *See also* Desert Wisdom Books bookstore; "Punks and Monks" Books
Boone, David, *Punkocalypse* 54 n.21
branch theory 37 n.22
Bunyan, John, *A Pilgrim's Progress* 32

Campus Crusade for Christ 80
Christensen, Hieromonk Damascene 43, 47, 56, 118
Christian/Christianity 31, 64–5, 67, 72–3, 77–8, 80–1, 85, 86 n.18, 92, 97, 99–100, 106 n.20, 107, 108 n.24, 109, 113, 116, 118. *See also* Antichrist
  acts-based Christianity 62
  catechumens 63, 65–6, 114

"Christian rock" 58, 108
"Christ is risen from the dead" (*Christos Anesti Ek Nekron*) 73
The Circle Jerks band 28
Cisneros, Al 30
Collins, John J. 48
   apocalyptic literature 48 n.10
commodification 15, 113
communion 39, 78 n.5, 88, 91, 108 n.24
communism 36 n.20, 43, 72, 77, 81–2, 84
Cone, James, *God of the Oppressed* 100 n.12
Congdon, David W. 49–50
conspiracy theory 4, 35, 50, 92, 95, 97, 102, 109–13
   9/11 "Trutherism" 110 n.26
constructive theology 4, 18
consumerism 15, 17, 22, 100
consumption and theology 4, 12–13, 16, 18, 29, 69–70, 96, 105
contemporary Christian music (CCM) 58
contemporary worship 62, 108 n.24
co-optation 100, 104, 117, 119
countercultures 3, 5, 15–16, 26–7, 37 n.23, 42–6, 52, 57, 61–3, 66, 70, 76, 97, 102, 113
Covid-19 pandemic 21, 72, 77, 85–91, 86 n.17, 102–3
Crissman, Marina 63, 65–6, 76
crucifixion 20, 33, 72–3
cultural Marxism 102. *See also* Marxism/Marxist

Dead Kennedys band, "Holiday in Cambodia" 104
#deathtotheworld 3, 76, 91
Death to the World 29–32, 34, 36–8, 36 n.20, 42–4, 46–52, 54, 61 n.2, 69–71, 73–7, 81–2, 84–8, 86 n.17, 91–7, 99–102, 104, 106–9, 108 n.24, 112–19
   "black and white" theo-asthetic 51, 112, 114
   Orthodoxy/Death T-shirt from 102–3
   "otherworldliness" 22, 75, 90–1, 94–5, 112
   Tsarism within 77, 82, 85

Death to the World (DTW) 4–11, 43–4, 47, 54–5, 54 n.21, 61–3, 65–6, 68–9, 72–3, 81, 86, 104
   antimodernism, exoticism, and politics 16
   inaugural issue of 8
   marketplace consumption and religious practice 12–15
   punk rock culture and consumerism 15–16
   sample page from zine 9
Death to the World En Español 73
democracy 83
demon/demonic 36, 56 n.24, 72, 84, 103, 109–11. *See also* Satan/Satanic/Satanism
The Descendants band 27
Desert Wisdom Books bookstore 115. *See also* bookstores
divine 2–3, 2 n.3, 11, 22, 48, 85, 88, 112
DIY reproducibility 42, 52, 68

Eastern Orthodox Christianity 3–5, 11–17, 34, 46, 48, 54 n.21, 61, 65, 67, 78, 80, 101, 113–14, 116
Eastern Orthodox monasticism 30
ecclesial/ecclesiology 3–4, 12, 14–15, 26, 31–2, 37 n.22, 58, 63, 67, 74, 76, 78, 80, 100, 102, 107 n.20, 108, 112
economy/economics 14 n.17, 41, 71, 87, 110–12, 117
Ecumenical Patriarch of Constantinople 14 n.18, 79–80
ecumenism 19, 36, 36 n.22, 74, 86 n.18, 110. *See also* anti-ecumenism
Ek Nekron podcast 73
emotions 20, 40, 63, 103, 110
Enlightenment 35, 35 n.19, 49, 83
eschatology, apocalyptic 35 n.17, 48–9, 109, 112
essentialism 32, 114. *See also* anti-essentialism
Estonian Orthodox church 79
ethics 2, 18, 22, 28, 30, 49, 51, 70, 97
Eucharist/Eucharistic 78–80, 105
Europe 7, 55, 71 n.20
evangelical/evangelicalism 26, 29, 48–9, 62–3, 65, 67, 73, 80
Evangelical Orthodox Church in America (EOC) 80

Facebook 9, 71, 87, 93
factionalism 116–17
Fear band 101
St. Febronia 52–3
501c3 nonprofit organization 75
Foucault, Michel 13, 67

Gerasim, Abbot 43, 65–6
gnostic/Gnosticism 111–12
God 8, 18, 20, 22, 33, 37, 39, 46, 51, 63, 87 n.18, 90, 98, 106–7, 109–10, 112, 119
God-ordained monarch 77, 82–3
Goff, Philip, *Religion and the Marketplace in the United States* 14 n.17
Goodfella's Tattoo Parlor in Orange, CA 62–3
goodness 2
Google 93
Great Council of Crete 14 n.18
Greek nationalism 74
Greek Orthodox Church in America (GOA) 7 n.10, 79
Griffiths, Paul J. 106–7
Grimm, Christian 74–5

hagiography 34, 43, 54–5, 75, 90–1, 103–4, 117
Han, Byung-Chul 87
Hart, David Bentley 15
Heimbach, Matthew 80
Herbel, D. Oliver 33
Herman, Abbott 41
St. Herman of Alaska Monastery in Platina, CA 5, 12, 17, 34, 36, 37 n.23, 38, 38 n.27, 41, 43, 56, 65–6, 68, 75
Hollinger, David 100, 100 n.10
"Holy Rus" 4, 85
Holy Scripture 86–7 n.18
Holy Spirit 15, 107
Hot Topic 105, 105 n.17
humanity 8, 12–13, 35, 44, 84, 86, 111, 113

identity formation 4, 13–14, 30, 69
immanent/immanence 21–2, 49–50, 97, 100, 102, 111–12
immigrants 14, 67, 79

independent churches. *See* autocephaly/autocephalous church
Instagram 9, 71
  "Banned Not Essential" from DttW Instagram 91
  "Immunity" from DttW Instagram 90
Institutional Review Board (IRB) policies 18
internet 4, 66–8, 71, 94, 106, 109
interpretations 20–1, 32, 49, 78, 113
St. Isaac the Syrian 6, 44, 99

Jacob 99
Jennings, Theodore W., Jr., *Outlaw Justice: The Messianic Politics of Paul* 99
Jerusalem 87 n.18
Jesus Christ 20, 26, 31–3, 63–5, 82, 97–9, 105, 107 n.20
"Jesus Christ Hardcore" 63
Jesus of Nazareth 99
Jews 87, 98
St. John Chrysostom 66, 83
St. John of Damascus 11, 106
Johnson, Buck 61 n.2
Jones, Alex, "Infowars" 110
Junker, Detlef, *Religion and the Marketplace in the United States* 14 n.17

Käsemann, Ernst 49, 49 n.12
"katechon" (τὸ κατέχον) 82, 84
Kiss ("Kids in Satan's Service") rock group 59 n.28

Laferney, Ryan Timothy 114–15
LGBTQIA+ community 113
Lincoln, Bruce 95
  Authority: Construction and Corrosion 66
liturgy/liturgical 34, 36, 39–40, 65–6, 79–80, 88, 109
lived religion 4, 11–14, 17, 20, 114
Lofton, Kathryn 13, 105
Lücke, Friedrich 48 n.10
Lynch, Zechariah 82–4

Macarius 6
MacKaye, Ian 30, 105

Marler, Justin 5, 5 n.5, 7–8, 8 n.11, 11, 12 n.15, 17, 26, 29–32, 36, 38–41, 43–4, 46, 48, 50–2, 54–8, 62, 62 n.3, 65–6, 69–70, 101, 105–6, 108, 114, 116
   early life of 26–7
   interviews of 26 n.3, 31 n.13, 58
   "Lamentations" 54
   love for God 33–4
   musical projects in punk 29 n.9
   on punk *vs.* monk lifestyle 5–6 n.6
   The Quick and the Dead project 58
   and religion 30–3
   "Unseen Warfare" website 9, 59
   Youth of the Apocalypse and the Last True Rebellion 54 n.21, 55, 57, 59, 63, 65
martyrdom 3, 7, 43, 52, 54, 81, 83–4, 103
Marxism/Marxist 36, 49, 77, 81–2, 84, 88, 102–3. *See also* anti-Marxism
   cultural Marxism 102
Marx, Karl 81 n.8
materiality 28–9, 33, 42, 106–7
Mathewes-Green, Frederica, *At the Corner of East and Now* 56, 65
Maximum Rocknroll zine 42, 52, 52 n.18
McGinn, Bernard 48, 51, 111
   invocation of "judgment" 49
McInroy, Mark 2, 3 n.4
memento mori 12, 21
merchandise 3, 8, 9–11, 30, 32, 61, 68, 71, 74, 105–6
Messiah 86–7 n.18, 99
metal scenes 3, 5, 7–8, 16, 23, 25, 29, 29 n.9, 41, 58, 68–9, 74–5, 101, 109, 114
military aesthetics 103
Minor Threat band 28, 30
modernity/modernism 4–5, 16, 19, 21, 27, 51, 101, 112. *See also* antimodernism/antimodernist
monarchy/monarchism 36 n.20, 77, 81–3
monastery/monastic/monasticism 5–8, 7 n.10, 16–17, 30, 34, 36, 39–44, 46, 54, 56–8, 65–6, 71, 74–5, 102, 116
   Eastern Orthodox monasticism 30
monks 5–7, 17, 31, 36, 40–1, 43–6, 55, 57, 65–6, 71, 104, 116
Moscow Patriarchate 14 n.18, 79

Naked Raygun band 27
neoliberal capitalism 13, 70, 78
New Age 8, 36, 62
Newman, John Henry 15
Newsome, Gavin 93, 112 n.30
New Testament 49 n.12, 50
New World Order 4, 34, 81–2, 85–6, 88, 92–3, 95, 109–10
Nietzsche, Friedrich 37–8, 47, 55
   "madman in the marketplace," *The Gay Science* 37–8
nihilism/nihilistic 3, 5, 7, 12, 16, 21, 34–8, 41, 43–6, 55, 60, 74, 82, 97, 99
   Rose's invocations of 36, 52, 55
9/11 "Trutherism" 110 n.26
St. Nikephoros the Leper 91
Nikodemus, Elder 44, 69
nothingness 45
Not of This World 45, 56, 73

Occult 8, 52, 62, 70
OM band, "God is Good" 30
Open Bible, Los Angeles 63
Oriental Orthodox 78 n.5
Orthodox Christian Studies Center at Fordham University 74
Orthodox Church in America (OCA) 7 n.10, 79–80
Orthodox/Orthodoxy 3–6, 11–16, 14 n.18, 18–19, 18 n.26, 22, 32–4, 35 n.18, 36, 38–9, 41–4, 46–7, 51, 54 n.21, 55, 57–9, 59 n.28, 61 n.2, 62–3, 65, 68–70, 72–81, 83, 85–6, 87 n.18, 88, 99 n.8, 101–2, 106–9, 112, 114, 116–17, 118–19
   Oriental Orthodox 78 n.5
   Orthodox Christians/Christianity 12, 35, 52, 58, 59 n.28, 77, 80, 84, 92, 95
   Orthodox Church 2, 12, 39, 43, 96, 107, 115
   Orthodox monasticism 46
   Orthodox Pascha 73
   Orthodox Tsar (Byzantine and Russian) 83–4
   Russian Orthodox/Orthodoxy 34, 81–3
   US Eastern Orthodoxy (*see* US Eastern Orthodoxy)
   zealot Orthodoxy 118

Orthodox Unlimited designer 9, 37 n.22.
See also 13th Vigil designer
Byzantine war flag in shirts of 10 n.13
slogans 74
The Orthodox Word magazine 43, 66, 81
otherworldliness 22, 75, 90–1, 94–5, 112

Pagels, Elaine 109–10
St. Paisios Abbey in Forestville, CA
54 n.21, 86 n.18, 92–3, 95
Parent, Joseph 92
parishes 14, 44, 57, 66, 69, 71, 72 n.21,
79–80, 88, 107
Pärt, Arvo 19
Patitsas, Timothy 1–2, 2 n.3, 22
Patriarch of Constantinople 14 n.18, 79
Pattton, Raymond A. 28
perpetual rebellion 22, 32, 47, 50–1. *See also* rebel/rebellion
Podmonshensky, Herman 34
Protestant/Protestantism 29, 32, 49, 54
n.21, 62–3, 66, 73–4, 80, 88, 106
n.20
punk 3–8, 12, 12 n.15, 15–17, 19, 22–3,
26–7, 38–9, 41–2, 45–7, 51–2, 54,
57–8, 62–3, 65, 68–70, 74–5, 77,
82, 95, 99 n.8, 100–2, 104–6, 109,
112–17
as lifestyle 27–9
Marler's musical projects in 29 n.9
punk protest 96
punk textuality 28, 41, 69
"Punks and Monks" Books 56, 75, 107
n.22. *See also* bookstores
Punx 45
Putin, Vladimir 96

Qualls, Turbo 61–6, 61 n.2, 70, 86 n.17

The Ramones band 27–8
rebel/rebellion 29, 32, 38–9, 44–7, 51,
55, 69–70, 72–4, 77, 81, 88, 95, 97,
99, 114, 119. *See also* perpetual rebellion
religious studies 17
Renaissance 35, 35 n.19
"Resist the New World Order" 75
resurrection 20, 33, 73, 98–9, 104–5
revelation 15, 47–9

Roman Catholics/Catholicism 49, 59, 80,
88, 107
Romanian Orthodox church 14 n.18, 79
The Romanov family 21, 36 n.20, 81, 102
Romans 5–6 98
Romans 6:3-11 97
Romans 13 98
Roof, Wade Clark 78
Rorschach test 23, 92
Rosa, Hartmut, age of acceleration 66
Rose, Seraphim 3, 5, 7–8, 7 n.10, 16, 21,
34–5, 37–8, 41, 43, 46–7, 50–2, 54,
56, 68, 72, 74–5, 77, 81, 92–3, 95,
101, 107, 109, 112, 112 n.30, 115,
117–19
critique of Marx 81 n.8
invocations of nihilism 36, 52, 55
"Living the Orthodox Worldview"
58–9 n.28
Nihilism: The Root of the Revolution of the Modern Age 36
"The Orthodox Survival Course"
35 n.18, 37 n.23, 71, 110
popular culture 43, 58 n.28
"The Soul after Death" 71
"super-correctness" 118
Rotten, Johnny 28, 64
Russian Orthodox Church Outside of
Russia (ROCOR) 7 n.10, 14 n.18
Russia/Russian 5, 34, 41, 43, 73, 79, 81,
84–5, 88, 94, 102
Russian Orthodox church 14 n.18, 79
Russian Orthodox/Orthodoxy 34, 81–3

sacraments/sacramental 88, 91, 94
sainthood 88, 107
salvation 48, 54 n.21, 91, 98, 106
samizdat 35 n.18, 43
Sandy Hook Elementary School in
Newtown, CN, tragic shootings
110
Satan/Satanic/Satanism 59, 84, 87, 87 n.18.
See also demon/demonic
schism of Rome 35 n.18
Schumacher, Owen 73
Scream Destroy Riot 93
Scupoli, Lorenzo 59
secularized apocalypse 112
St. Seraphim of Sarov 47

Sex Pistols band 27–8, 99 n.8
  "Anarchy in the U.K." 28
  "No Future" 99
sin 20, 59, 98, 111
Skete, Theophany 56–7, 116
Sleep band 5, 25–6, 29, 31, 40, 57, 75
  "Anguish" 25
  "Dopesmoker" 25
  "Scourge" 25
  "Stillborn" 25–6
  "The Suffering" 25
  Volume 1 25–6, 29
social media 3, 9, 67, 71, 76, 93–4, 115. *See also specific companies*
sociology 17
sonic cultures 4, 16, 19, 29, 69, 113
soteriology 20, 98
spirit 32, 45, 59, 65, 71–2, 75, 97, 112, 117, 119
spiritual/spirituality 2–7, 3 n.4, 13, 17, 19, 26–32, 35–6, 41, 43, 45–6, 51–2, 55–9, 62–3, 70–1, 74–6, 84, 88, 90–1, 93–4, 96–7, 99–100, 102, 104–7, 112
  spiritual hospital 66
  spiritual vigilance 117
  spiritual warfare 35, 43, 51–2, 75, 111
Stein, Matt 56, 115–17
Stievermann, Jan, *Religion and the Marketplace in the United States* 14 n.17
Stith, Deborah Sengupta, "The Unbroken Circle" 58 n.26
stoner metal 5, 25
straight edge 15, 30–1, 95, 102
subcultures 4–5, 12, 16, 23, 29, 51, 56 n.24, 57–8, 61 n.2, 69–70, 74–6, 95, 101, 108–9, 114–16
  youth 41, 105 n.17, 115
supernatural 48, 50–1, 111

Temple of Solomon 87 n.18
theo-aesthetics 2–4, 2 n.3, 11, 18, 20–2, 43, 46, 68, 74, 76, 97, 104, 109–14, 119
Theophany 2
theo-politics/political 84–5, 88, 94, 102, 104

13th Vigil designer 9, 37 n.22, 70, 74–5. *See also* Orthodox Unlimited designer
Thompson, Stacy 28, 41, 69
St. Timothy Antiochian Orthodox Church in Lompoc, CA 17, 71
tomos (certificate of autocephaly) 79
Toop, David 16, 69
totalitarian/totalitarianism 34, 36, 82
transcendent/transcendence 1–2, 48, 50, 54, 104
transgression 99
truth 1–3, 31–2, 45, 50–1, 55, 82, 96, 99, 108, 115–16, 119
  and embodiment 32–3
Tsakiridou, C. A. 2 n.3
Tsarhood (the monarch) 82
Tsarism 77, 82, 85
  Tsarist monarchy 81–5
Tsar Nicholas 2 21, 36 n.20, 81, 84, 96
Twitter 93
2 Thessalonians 82–3

Ukraine 85
  Ukrainian Orthodox Church 79
The United States 3–5, 7, 9, 11–12, 14–15, 14 n.18, 21, 29, 41, 43, 55, 57, 67, 73–4, 77, 79–81, 85, 100, 100 n.10, 114, 119. *See also* US Eastern Orthodoxy
"Unite the Right" rally (2017) 80
Uscinski, Joseph E. 92
US Eastern Orthodoxy 3–5, 7 n.10, 11–14, 23, 30, 68, 72, 79–80, 97
  authority in 76–81

Valadez, John 1, 8–9, 11, 12 n.15, 17, 42, 44, 56, 58, 61–6, 62 n.3, 68–73, 75, 99, 101, 106, 108, 114, 117, 119
  "bait on a hook" 44, 114, 117
Viata parintelui Iustin Pirvu spiritual text 88–9

Watts, Alan 36
Wermuth, Andrew, *Youth of the Apocalypse and the Last True Rebellion* 55, 59

white supremacy/supremacist 15, 78, 80, 95
World Council of Churches-level collaboration 37 n.22
Wuthnow, Robert 67
Wu, Tim 71
  The Attention Merchants: The Epic Scramble to Get inside Our Heads 71 n.20

"Youth of the Apocalypse Conference" 54 n.21
zealotry 118
Zen Buddhism 36
zines 3, 7–8, 11–12, 19, 22–3, 28, 34, 41–4, 47, 51–5, 54 n.21, 57, 59, 61–6, 68–9, 71, 73–4, 76–7, 82, 86–7, 89, 103, 106–7, 115
Zionism/Zionists 86, 86–7 n.18

www.ingramcontent.com/pod-product-compliance
Lightning Source LLC
Chambersburg PA
CBHW051527230426
43668CB00012B/1772